ANOTHER KIND OF ORDINARY

(Living with Autism, Learning Difficulties and Aggression: the Story of a Mother's Love)

First published 2017

Printed by 4edge Publishing
22 Eldon Way
Eldon Way Industrial Estate
Hockley Essex SS5 4AD

Preface

As a secondary school teacher expecting my third child, I thought I knew what to expect from motherhood and how to deal with most situations. However, I was totally unprepared for what followed as I embarked on a course where past experience was irrelevant and no systems were effective. These are the events that followed and my reflections on my new life.

It is my story but it is also the story of many mothers living with similar challenges - some of whom you will meet in your daily lives. There are no answers yet, only increasing understanding that comes through shared experience.

This book tells my story from pregnancy to the approach of Ben's eighteenth birthday. It is divided into five parts: a series of (roughly chronological) anecdotes for parts one to three; my personal reflections on different issues in part four and a look to the future in part five.

Dedication

This book is dedicated to my husband and three children who have lived this story with me.

Acknowledgements

I wish to thank my mother for her enthusiasm for this book and for being my confidante throughout the difficulties and triumphs of life; my friend Sheila for her honesty and frank comments on reading my first draft, her encouragement to pursue publication and her deepening friendship, and my friend Jan for being there for me in life's toughest moments. Their support to me has been invaluable.

I am also grateful to Malcolm, Karen and Tim for their help with the cover photographs; to Paul for his publishing advice and to Ian for his cover design, text layout, and his patience with my many revisions.

Finally, my thanks go to my husband, for being an amazing soul-mate and father, and to my three sons who together make this family what it is.

Author's Note

To protect my son's identity, names of key figures in this story have been changed. Identifying names of places and other individuals have also been omitted. Where possible, to the best of my knowledge, permission has been obtained from individuals and groups alluded to in this book.

ANOTHER KIND OF ORDINARY

*(Living with Autism, Learning Difficulties and Aggression:
the Story of a Mother's Love)*

By
Pam Cottle

Contents

PART 1

In the Beginning...

CHAPTER 1

In the Beginning...Tests!

When we enter into an agreement with God and Nature to produce a human being the guarantee of health and wholeness is never offered on the documentation. Nor is there a returns policy for defective items. This belongs to the parallel world of consumerism and finance. It does not stop us testing the product from the moment the order is confirmed. What are you supposed to do with the tiny baby who fails one of many evaluations of its fragile life? This is no defective machine. This is a precious son, daughter, brother, sister, grandchild.

Do you wish to have the amniocentesis test, Mrs Cottle? The midwife asked the question with almost no pause for reply. For mothers of my age, she already knew what to write.

"No thank you," I replied with a shocking certainty, "But I will have the blood test."

Two images had imprinted themselves on my mind - one of a dear friend who had lost a baby after amniocentesis. She suffered a terrifying ordeal in a foreign hospital, losing her unborn child in a mist of interpreters and white-cloaked ministers of death and life. The other was of a brave forty-something lady who refused all tests then woke to the unforeseen nightmare of giving birth to a needy child to whose care she would devote the remainder of her life. Richard and I had no intention of aborting our unborn child. We *did* want to prepare ourselves for 'any eventuality'. The results were normal. Our baby had passed the preliminary test!

Actually, my son passed his first evaluation at birth with an impressive score. He was perfect, healthy, beautiful, loved. A loud, inaudible sigh was released by those around who had dared to believe an alternative outcome possible. Welcome to the world - a first class honours for your first examination!

The next twelve months disappeared in a haze of hectic life. Ben did not sleep through the night in this first year; neither had my older children. No alarm. Ben grew as the charts decreed. He could hear. The first sets of inoculations were completed. He crawled and walked at the right time. He passed another important examination. No alarm - just the normal hard work that babies bring and the challenge to accommodate this within the pre-existing framework of our family life.

Having a baby when all my close friends were eagerly embracing the next stage in the life-cycle was at once rejuvenating and ageing. I mixed with younger, inexperienced mums; joined mums and tots' groups and frequented baby wear and toy departments. I also competed on the secondary schools' circuit and ran mum's transport arrangements as social activities a-plenty engulfed my calendar on behalf of my other children. My breast-fed baby accompanied me everywhere, enjoying his succour at any hour and many locations, as discretion and necessity decreed. Ordinary life was always about maintaining a functional harmony within this machine of many moving parts. It was about embracing and enjoying the perpetual motion, but this was no mechanical empire: it was a family and what kept it moving was caring, talking and engaging together. It still does!

CHAPTER 2

The Speech Therapist and the 'A' word

At a routine developmental test, Ben failed a key section. Crawling - tick - progress - good. Walking - tick - progress - good. Talking - cross. Progress - poor. Question mark.

"Your son's speech development is a little delayed. It's probably nothing to worry about but I will come back and see you in a few weeks and re-test. Try not to worry! It's probably nothing." With such hollow assurance, the health visitor disappeared to attend her next appointment. Failure. We had not reached the required standard. My response to failure is to try harder. I redoubled my efforts to read, sing and talk to Ben. I mouthed words to him, trying to evoke a mimicked reply. Success was limited but some was evidenced. I told myself not to worry and tried harder. We had to pass this test together!

At her next visit, we had apparently made inadequate progress.

She suggested a referral to a small group therapy session with a speech therapist.

"It will be fun, based around playing games. It might be just the boost he needs to catch up. It is a helping hand, a gentle push in the right direction. It is a great new initiative to give early support to young children to deal with problems before school age."

"Early intervention," I thought. I was familiar with the concept.

I remembered the son of a friend who had benefitted from speech therapy some years before. He went on to win a place at an academic school and overcame his early issues. I felt reassured.

"Of course, I am happy to put our names forward for the program."

When we arrived, we were greeted by an older lady with a brisk, officious manner. She explained carefully but firmly that the parents were invited to view the proceedings from an adjacent room with a two-way mirror. The toddlers were whisked off to 'play their games and have fun.' Inevitably both the children and the parents were uneasy and agitated to begin with. It required much coaxing and an uncompromising stare from the official to prise the parents and the children from each other. What followed was a series of shape-sorting activities and other simple games with brightly-coloured toys and puzzles, initiated by verbal instructions, at times requiring individual verbal responses.

There were three children in this group. The first was pretty, attentive and produced mostly correct answers. She received frequent praise and seemed to be the teacher's pet. The second was uncooperative and restless but produced the right responses when he concentrated. He received great praise when he applied himself and overcame his evident issues with attention. Ben tried hard but seemed lost, confused. He rarely seemed to elicit praise. He looked disappointed, dejected, withdrawn.

From the outset, I felt something was wrong about the way this situation was handled. The repeated approval given to one individual and its contrast with the total lack of encouragement for another contradicted everything I knew and believed in both personally and professionally in my job as a teacher, especially as these children were assembled here precisely because of concerns raised. The approach I witnessed here would not be acceptable in the world of education. It would not be advocated by any child agency. Something was wrong with the process.

At the end of the last session, the person in charge saw each mother individually. There was no preamble in our conversation. No attempt to prepare me for what she said, no aftercare. Just the single shot from close range, then the door.

"I think your child is autistic. I shall refer you for on-going individual speech therapy and to a paediatric consultant who will be able to make a formal diagnosis."

I took Ben's hand and left, outwardly composed, polite. Inside I staggered, crumpled and fell, like the victim in a murder story. No words, no witnesses - just a body, lifeless, still. Silence. For a moment, I died. Then it was as if I refused to yield to the cold stillness of death and returned not to my old life but as a new individual, with a new purpose and a changed destiny.

"I love you," I whispered, as I embraced Ben with a mother's love.

As I drove home, I reminded myself that this woman was not qualified to diagnose autism as she was a speech therapist, not a doctor.

She also clearly had little understanding of psychology or compassion. I was angry that she had assumed a responsibility that was not hers. I was indignant that she had done this with so little feeling.

On arriving home, I settled Ben, then immediately sat in front of my computer. Autism - what is autism? What does it mean? What are the characteristics? What treatments are available? Is there a cure? What causes it? Is there a hereditary link? At moments like this, thoughts do not come neatly and in single file, they charge at you like an angry mob - each one craving recognition over the next, jostling for superiority in your brain. I scanned websites, compared findings and soaked up information. The results did not bring clarity to my situation. Ben did not fit the classic triad of impairments they defined. There were elements I recognised in him but the puzzle did not fit well. Gaining answers to my queries seemed only to produce more questions. I was unconvinced.

So in fact were the experts in the Paediatric team at my local hospital. They hedged, they did more tests, they discussed with their wider panel of supporting ministries. We went from appointment to appointment, in obedience to their call: speech therapist, occupational therapist, paediatrician, health visitor but every appointment failed to bring any conclusion, rather raising more uncertainty. Then one day the consultant bravely told us the truth. She was not sure. She did not know. She was referring us to a specialist diagnostic centre a hundred miles away for an assessment by experts in this field for a second opinion. We were surprised. It was not what Richard and I had expected to hear but I deeply admired her for her courage. I have never despised lack of knowledge, only doubt expressed as truth, especially when that doubt is presented as expert opinion. Thank you, I thought, for your honesty. The verdict was still open in this case.

CHAPTER 3

The Court Case

The visit to the diagnostic centre was a major expedition. It involved a full day out, leaving early for the hour and a half journey traversing a monotonous motorway until finally we steered off the commuter frenzy and into a quiet rural landscape. The centre resembled more a small boarding school or a forgotten sanatorium than a clinic. We entered by a long driveway, passing through wild flower hedges and wooded glades. The large grey stone house was deserted but for a few key workers and a maze of empty rooms and corridors. We were greeted politely at the door and invited to a waiting area with toys to fill in a few forms. Ben was then taken from the newly-found toys and us by two kindly strangers to have a series of assessments. We walked out with them but were told we could see where they were going and the first few puzzle tests but then it would be better if we left. Ben would be brought back to us afterwards.

It seemed so unnatural to take a young child away from his parents, in the company of complete strangers and ask him to do a series of unusual activities that he would probably find difficult. Not for the first time, I felt I was placed in a position of being blackmailed into doing something unnatural, contrary to all my maternal instincts of protection, comfort, support. When would you ever let a three-year old disappear with two people you did not know? I could not even prepare him by giving him time to get to know these strangers or by informing him in advance about the things he would be asked to do. Any child would struggle to display their abilities under such strange and pressured conditions, yet the results of these tests might substantially affect his future. We now felt controlled by a system that we had entered voluntarily; forced to trust people we did not know. Helpless! Trapped!

Ben was returned to us between the tests and at the end we were presented with their verdict...

It was again inconclusive. Case adjourned for twelve months. Re-appear in the courtroom in twelve months' time! It might be a speech problem - in which case he may grow out of it - or it could be autistic spectrum disorder but they wanted to leave the verdict open at this stage; they did not want to place a large label on his neck until they were sure. They did, however, assist us with letters to the education department with strong recommendations of support needed. You felt they were trying to help. They were honest. They were unsure. We left that day half-elated, half-disappointed, totally exhausted, no further on...

During this time, Ben met regularly with a new speech therapist. She was kind and gentle and Ben enjoyed doing the activities she prepared for him but little change was evidenced and eventually these visits ceased.

A year later we returned. This time we were expectant, quiet, reflective, familiar now with the journey and the day's prospect and certain that by the end of it we would at least have clarity. I remember little of the second visit. I remember only the concluding remarks:

"We feel that Ben's difficulties are more likely to be related to the autistic spectrum than purely speech and language based but as he clearly does not display some of the typical features of autistic spectrum disorder, your son is not easy to diagnose…"

In a way, I think they had made their decision but because of the element of ambiguity still remaining, we agreed on a further delay. They suggested a final appointment for twelve months' time when a decision would be reached. That appointment never took place. When I contacted them to arrange it, I was told that my local health authority no longer had links with their centre. The case would not be heard again in this court. The awaited verdict was not to be given for a number of years, under very different circumstances.

Perhaps I knew deep down what they were trying to say to us from the second encounter; how if we had not pressed them, they might have given their diagnosis at that time. Perhaps I was not ready then to accept this truth. Sometimes as parents you have to be in a certain place to receive unwelcome news. Sometimes there is a right time to hear, even if you know long before!

CHAPTER 4

Tantrums, Dark Nights and the Blue Rinse Ladies

Toddlers have tantrums. I knew that - I had raised two older sons. Tantrums are embarrassing, difficult to deal with, but necessary. Through them, a child learns that his will has to be subjected to external boundaries. He is not a despot whose rule is absolute. He is not the centre of the universe, around which all the planets in his solar system rotate. Through this process, a toddler learns the skills to become a social being, a part in a larger whole. During this period, toddlers display a disproportionate degree of egocentricity, manipulation and exhibitionism. Ultimately, through this process, they learn the skills to adapt and thrive in the human community.

My memories of this period included many dark, cold evenings when in desperation, I placed Ben screaming in his pushchair and walked, in the wind and the rain, silently, aimlessly, soundless tears rippling down my shielded face. I did not know what else to do. It was the only possibility to protect his older siblings and afford them the opportunity to sleep. I never met anyone, at least I never saw anyone. I never spoke, except to attempt to soothe him. I prayed many desperate prayers. I followed the same aimless route - a suburban nothingness of dreary pavements and locked front doors. It was then that I first experienced the numbness that comes with knowing you have tried all the ideas you have and failed; that there is nothing left to try, yet the problem remains. Finally, exhaustion gave Ben up to sleep. My life resumed.

....

The planners of a large department store in my vicinity had located the children's department in the basement. They had created a large enclosed space and they had thought of everything: there was a lift; there were stairs; they had helpful assistants who might have had children themselves. They also placed other departments within this space, frequented by individuals of a senior generation who enjoyed strolling at their leisure around the wares as an amiable way of passing their abundant time. It was into this enclosed space that I stepped one morning with my pushchair, unaware of the incarceration I would soon experience there.

Doubtless unimpressed by the need to survey the endless racks of merchandise, my toddler began his tirade. I remember only cameos of this memorable event. I recall much shouting, screaming and flailing from Ben, breaching the convention of silence and composure in this majestic stronghold. I recall the eyes of voyeurs peering at a safe distance with disdain and incredulity and their whispered murmurs of extreme disapproval. I received the contempt on behalf of every younger person for the failings of our generation.

Ben arched his back, like an angry prisoner determined to shake off the hated shackles of his pushchair restraint.

A kindly shop assistant approached, fearful but willing, "Is he having a fit?" she stammered, her fear increasingly overcoming her professionalism. "Is there anything I can do?" She backed away slightly, commencing her retreat.

"He is not having a fit. He is having a tantrum," I replied firmly, by way of communicating the simple fact to her. "No, I don't think there is anything you can do, thanks."

The relief on her face was evident. Her intent had been positive. She had not failed in her professional duty. In declining her offer, I had released her from her responsibility and she was thankful.

Instead, I vented a little of my frustration on the blue-rinse ladies.

"Please don't stare. It doesn't help!"

The two hawks lifted their gaze and flew off, in disgust.

With great effort and much noise, I made my way to the lift, the only exit from this prison block. I had to wait forever whilst the lift, an officious guard, unwilling to accept our release papers, whirred and hissed, ignoring my desperate pleas for haste. As prisoners awaiting release, those final minutes hung in suspension seemed as long as the total hours of confinement. Eventually we gulped the fresh air of the open street. We were back in the free world!

My son's tantrums were frequent and extreme. "It will pass," I thought. "All toddlers go through this phase. It will get better. Hang on in there! Stick to your principles! Success is assured: in the end, change is inevitable! A phase, no more," I comforted myself. "A few more months and he will be starting playgroup. A new environment will help. It will pass." But these moments did not pass. I began to keep a log. Could I find a causal link? Food intolerance? Feeling unwell? I could not. Surely it will pass?

CHAPTER 5

Playgroup and the Magic Key

I had booked a place for Ben from an early age at a local playgroup recommended by neighbours. I had not questioned their judgement since its proximity made it the convenient choice. As he was approaching the age to start they contacted me to arrange a visit. I duly escorted him, having explained roughly what to expect: painting, play dough, trains and cars, sand, kind helpers and new friends. We approached the building with a healthy mix of excitement and trepidation. As a mum, I knew this would be an important first step in the long road to independence both for him and myself; a landmark in the parenting process.

The playgroup was held in an old stone church hall up a steep flight of steps. Inside, the room was brightly decorated, if ill-lit from the high windows whose job seemed to be withholding light rather than allowing it entrance. There were many toys arranged in themed areas, busy children in bright coloured playwear and different activities supervised by helpers dressed in identical tabards. The scene was characterised by a combination of loud noise including high-pitched infant voices and strange mechanical noises emitting from various playthings. We were welcomed and invited to join in with the other children. After some hesitation, I steered Ben towards the train set and we began to play. The other children eyed us suspiciously and proceeded to play around us as if we were invisible.

After a short while a signal was given and the toys were duly packed away. A circle of chairs was formed in the centre of the room and the children filled them expectantly. Circle time meant having a drink and a biscuit followed by a time of singing songs and they clearly looked forward to it. We took our place in the circle and when everyone was both seated and quiet, the biscuit box was circulated by the chosen helper. Under the keen eye of the playgroup leader, the tin was offered to each child in turn on the condition that each child said the magic words 'Please may I have a biscuit?' took only one, then completed the incantation with the words 'Thank you.' As the ritual continued and the box drew closer, I could foresee the crisis without having the power to alter events. When it reached Ben there was a stony silence. The offer of the tin was not extended as the hushed silence had broken the spell. Twenty pairs of accusing eyes said your behaviour is unacceptable; you will not be allowed a biscuit. In an attempt to dissipate the tension, I interjected, 'I'm sorry but he doesn't speak much and rarely outside of the family.' I cannot remember if he received a biscuit that day but it was evident that unless the magic words were uttered, he would not receive one during his time at this playgroup. Rules were rules and this one was absolute!

The remainder of our time there was brief and unremarkable. As I left, I happened to mention that for us the toilet training process was not yet achieved.

"Well, I'm sorry but we do not have the facilities to change nappies. That has to be completed before he could start. Our helpers are not expected to do that."

As we picked our way carefully down the difficult steps to the road outside, I knew Ben would not set foot in that hall again. My thoughts raced to my new challenge - to find another local playgroup that would welcome us. There were really only a few other possibilities within a reasonable distance from our home. I knew that in all probability these would have been filled long ago by organised mothers like myself, who had added their children's names while still a young baby.

I walked into the new playgroup, apologetic and expecting little. I explained my plight, including what had happened at the other group. I told the leader about Ben's limited speech and his failure yet to grasp toilet training. This lady knew that I had not chosen her facility first, that Ben had a few problems, that I was desperate. She was under no obligation to me whatever. She had every opportunity to refuse my request. She did not. The building was rather dreary and dark but the atmosphere more than made up for that. Ben was invited to sample a session, made very welcome, encouraged to join in but allowed the freedom to make his own choices. He was also given a biscuit with the others.

Ben spent two and a half years at this playgroup. He was assigned a special helper who cared for him; changing him when necessary, encouraging him to join in where he could, respecting his right to choose not to if he preferred. She was a grandmother and he felt secure with her. She provided a haven of familiarity in this vast theatre of confusion. He took his place in the nativity play and had his photograph in the paper when local sporting heroes came to visit. He did not like to be centre stage but enjoyed a parallel life on the fringes of the children's frenetic activity. I believe he was happy there, in his own way.

Towards the end of his time there, with the prospect of Big School approaching, we began to start the process of seeking extra support for him as his education progressed. By this stage, Ben was under the care of a paediatrician and a speech therapist. His playgroup leader was a former schoolteacher so she and I began the first of many forms, applications, phone calls and meetings to attempt to acquire the mystical documentation that would conjure up additional resources for him throughout his school career. The culmination of many weeks of planning was a meeting attended by an educational psychologist, a speech therapist, a key worker from playgroup, the playgroup leader, an LEA worker and myself. It was recommended that Ben be given a Statement of Special Educational Needs - the Magic Key to money and manpower. The proposal had to be approved at an LEA Panel Meeting soon afterwards. It was refused on the grounds that his latest playgroup report was too positive. Incredulous, the playgroup leader and I discussed the verdict. In with other papers, we had included the last report to parents, containing euphemisms of how he was making limited progress, cloaked in kind terms to protect us. Any professional might have read the subtext effectively. This panel had not.

I approached the playgroup leader with a request no mother should have to make:

"Could you please write a report stating all the things that Ben cannot do in relation to his peers? "

"I understand, of course," she replied, knowing what I was asking for was for facts couched in language so raw that no educational professional would write them to a parent: a totally negative account.

I don't remember if she actually advised me not to read the offending document. I know I should have submitted the letter unread. In fact, I read it, wept and submitted our case afresh with this new evidence. Nothing had changed. The information given in both documents was factually correct. The first was written by caring people for loving parents, the second by a machine for bureaucratic analysis. The original decision was overturned at the next Panel Meeting. We had our Magic Key!

CHAPTER 6

The Label

As part of the process of applying for a statement of educational needs, we were required to attend a medical assessment. This was entirely independent of the medical appointments we had in order to obtain a diagnosis and both the personnel and venues were unfamiliar. I had no idea what to expect from this visit except that I was hoping for support in our quest for additional help at school. No diagnosis of autism appeared on any paperwork received by that office which left me totally unprepared for the question posed nonchalantly as boxes were ticked on the paperwork on the doctor's agenda.

"Do you want me to write *autism* on the form?"

Involuntarily, I drew back. There was something unnatural about the question. I was a parent, in the presence of a medical professional, yet this doctor asked me what *I* wanted on the form.

After a few long seconds, I regained some inward composure.

"What is your professional opinion?"

He avoided the question and my gaze.

"Put it this way, it doesn't matter to me whether I state that your son has delayed speech and developmental issues or autism. However, if I write the word *autism*, you will receive much more help in his education."

I felt a sense of disdain, revulsion. Autism is a big label to put on someone's life. It would change people's perspective of this person for ever, yet here was someone playing with semantics. This was not how it should be.

My pride and sense of professionalism took over. Slowly, carefully, I gave my considered response.

"If you are sure that he is autistic, please write that on the form. If this is just about negotiating the system, my husband and I are both teachers; we are not afraid of dealing with the local education department. We will fight our battles without it."

He looked straight at me for a few seconds as if saying 'Good Luck - you will need it!' before writing 'delayed speech and development issues' on the form in front of him.

I left the consulting room with my son that day horrified, disgusted, confused, but sure I had made the right decision. I knew I could not accept a label from a doctor who himself was unsure of its appropriateness, simply to make life easier. I also realised how many parents would have made a different choice - through convenience or blind faith in the wearer of a white coat.

My son was finally diagnosed with autistic spectrum disorder seven years later and in that time, we battled long and hard with the education system but when it finally came, I believed in its validity. The interval had removed all trace of doubt. By then, I no longer had to contend with guilt that I might have accepted the wrong diagnosis. I do not regret what I did that day.

CHAPTER 7

Swimming Lessons

Perhaps it was an unflinching belief in the essential value of learning to swim and a sense of parental duty to make that happen that made me sign up to join a course of swimming lessons with Ben's playgroup. Or was I simply caught off-guard, living in a moment of other people's normality? Whatever my motives, or state of mind, I had signed up and paid the fees.

We were looking forward to Thursday lunchtimes as our little troupe made our way from the church hall to the swimming baths, some ten minutes' drive apart. Richard and I had often taken Ben to this swimming pool so he was used to both the environment and water. Optimism. Normality.

After a few weeks of Ben clinging terrified to the side, failing to join in the activities and songs, a mixture of child-friendly ploys to entice toddlers to develop confidence and pre-swimming skills, I made a suggestion.

"Do you think it would help if I came in the water with my son?"

The teacher hesitated long enough to convey that this would contravene the usual guidelines but she was a kind, understanding lady, a mother and a playgroup helper. She could see that this was no ordinary case and she wanted to help. She was willing to lay down her textbook guidelines to do so.

"Yes, I think it might be worth a try."

The next week, I duly donned my own costume and slipped quietly into the water with him. Together, we tried to join in the activities, an adjunct to the group, deluding myself that we were actually part of it. For me, it gave a welcome escape from the camaraderie of friendly mums whose daily experiences I did not share. However, I had escaped one sense of isolation only in exchange for a visual and social difference greater than any that might have been excused by perceived shyness or preoccupation on my part. By the end of term, we participated in most of the activities alongside the others, always on the end of the line, always dependent on Ben's voluntary compliance that day. Progress had been made, however, and we anticipated that after the holidays we would continue that trend. We had not anticipated the announcement:

"Unfortunately, this is my last lesson with you all as I am leaving so you will have a new teacher next term. I am sure you will get on well with her. I shall tell her what clever children you are and how well you are doing with your swimming. Have a good holiday!"

"What a shame," I thought, "just as we were making progress."

"Thank you so much," I said with genuine warmth. "All the best with your new job! Have a good holiday!"

I left with the other mums, discussing the news, expressing our appreciation of this particular lady and curious to know who might take her place.

The first lesson after the holidays arrived with little further thought throughout the busy holiday period. I packed our two lots of swimming gear and met up as arranged with a congenial lady I did not know well. She was the grandmother of one of the other toddlers who had kindly offered to give us a lift that day since I did not have a car. We arrived with plenty of time, having chatted amicably about family life - the children, holidays and the cold weather. We made our way to the changing rooms already beginning to bustle with mums, toddlers and pushchairs jostling for space with the previous class's children dripping and darting in the narrow space. The odour of chlorine and warm bodies contrasted with the harsh cold outside. We found a space for our bags, removed our shoes and socks, then with Ben in my arms I moved out into the pool area where the new teacher, clipboard in hand was waiting for our class.

"Hello, I am Ben's mum. I'm not sure if you are aware but Ben has special needs and I have been coming into the pool with the class to help him to gain confidence and join in."

"*I know all about teaching special needs children.* I have done courses on this. It will not be necessary for you to come in. He will be fine, thank you."

The final thank-you was more of a command to stay away than an expression of any gratitude. I suppose the nature of dealing with the twin dangers of children and water predisposes swimming teachers to being authoritative and unbending with loud, booming voices but her demeanour was of the tough, no messing, 'do-as-I-say' style - a combination of arrogance and control. I felt an instant sense that this would not work out well, a dark rain-filled grey of impending doom. Sadly, I did not act on my instincts and paid dearly for doing so.

I turned to Ben, trying to sound convincing when I explained that he was going to be very grown up today and go into the pool without me like the other children. I handed him, already beginning to develop signs of distress, over to the teacher. At first, he was reluctant to get in the water. When he finally did so, he clung onto the side, too frightened to move or speak. I watched for some tense moments, telling myself I had to give it a try but after a while, my sense of guilt overwhelmed me and I walked poolside and lifted him shivering and terrified out of the water into the safety of my arms. She didn't object. She said nothing but stared blankly before continuing the lesson with the rest of the class. By now, Ben had begun to scream and shout; his arms and legs flailing wildly. This was a toddler tantrum with no limits, driven by fear, out of control.

I was in a small changing cubicle with a solid floor and hard sides. He was wild, angry, wet and constantly moving. My first thought was how easy it would be for him to hit his head and add physical pain and injury to this rapidly worsening scenario. How could I stop him hurting himself? Soon the class finished and the changing rooms filled with people. I felt ostracised, trapped as I was in this confined space between the hardness of the physical environment and the concentrated gaze of so many other mothers - incredulous, protective of their own children, unable to help. Most thankfully made their escape, some fearful, others looking back with expressions of disbelief or pity.

In the constant motion, I felt a hand on my shoulder, a voice in my ear:

"I understand, my sister has a child with difficulties."

I dared not turn around; I had my eyes firmly on Ben and my attempts to protect his head. I have never discovered the person behind that voice. 'Thank you, whoever you are, for a thread of intimacy, empathy in the battlefield under fire. It gave me a momentary glimpse of hope and the strength to keep going.'

As the crowded changing room emptied, I heard the swimming pool manager come and offer me assistance - not the genuine assistance of practical help but an expression of urgency intended to quickly rid his establishment of this public nuisance. I turned and there was the grandmother who had brought me in her car. Ben was now moderately dry but still shouting and totally refusing to put on any clothes. I cannot remember what was written in her eyes, but the fact that she was still there gave me the courage to ask:

"Would you be willing to drive me home please, if I wrap him up in a towel?"

So, with eager encouragement from the management, we left the swimming pool with Ben undressed, wrapped up in a towel, bundled like some criminal into her waiting car. Within a few minutes, the fear lifted, the aggression dissipated and my little boy, writhing only minutes before, snuggled into my arms, gently weeping.

"Thank you! Thank you so much!" I said as she dropped us at our front door, these familiar words inadequate to express the depth of feeling I wanted to convey. I held him, dressed him, watched him slowly come back to life and promised myself I would never let him near *that woman* again.

Exhausted and scarred, I determined that I would teach him to swim myself. I did and we often swim together in local swimming pools, even on occasions in *that* pool, the trauma of that day apparently long-forgotten for him, but not for me!

47

CHAPTER 8

The Childminder

For the first time in my life, when my youngest child was around three years of age I employed a professional childminder. I had always used friends with my other children, often with reciprocal arrangements. This time around, my long-standing friends were either back working or leading very busy lives. Whilst a few would do the occasional school pick-up, none were looking for a more serious commitment. I had the offer of an interesting job, working part-time, on a temporary contract. I decided it was time to do what every other working mother seemed to do and find a childminder. The one I approached was not unknown to me and I had seen at first hand at the local mums and tots group her care for other charges. We discussed the hours, signed the forms, everything was sorted. At the time, whilst I knew that Ben was not the easiest charge, I had no idea of the nature or severity of his difficulties and I thought the greater opportunity to mix with other children would be helpful. I knew it would take time to settle and was not alarmed at the difficult separations we experienced in the early weeks. For the first time, Richard shared the task of dropping him off before work and I was aware he found this stressful. We believed the situation would sort itself out. The childminder had several other children. Ben was young enough to play in an adjacent orbit as young children do but did not often engage with them. Inevitably, I think the childminder found the others easier to handle. She tried her best. She found him different from the others. She was not unkind or unfair. She was unprepared and unhappy.

I knew things had begun to unravel. Neither Ben, nor the childminder were happy. We hated taking him to her house and leaving him there. I had around a month to the end of my contract. I did not know what to do. We hung on, worried but trapped with no alternative but to cling on to the status quo. The breaking point arrived one evening as I picked him up. It felt cruel persevering with this situation that everyone knew was not working. I arrived on the doorstep of a dear friend and poured out my dilemma.

She was the only person I could think of who might be able to help. I knew she would understand. I knew she would love him and care for him. I also I knew she was not looking for work, that her life was already busy. I asked anyway.

"Would you be willing to look after him for the next few weeks while I finish out my contract?"

She was. The next day, the childminder greeted me with a week's notice to terminate my contract. This was waived when I told her I already had someone else who would start immediately. The sadness and relief on both sides was evident. I have rarely met her since.

In those few weeks, my friend nurtured Ben back to a state of being less distressed, less distant, less frightened, more secure. Her contribution to his wellbeing far exceeded the time spent working for me. It made us realise that we could not treat him just like any other toddler; that time spent individually would be required for him to progress; that what was suitable for many children was not going to suffice.

Sometime later, I was offered the perfect job doing what I loved with part-time hours and close to our home. By then I knew I could not accept it; I had a higher priority. How could I put my efforts into teaching other people's children when my own child needed me more? I wrote to the Headmistress, explaining why I could not accept her kind offer, explaining that I would rather refuse the post than not do it justice, that it was precisely because I knew and understood the demands of the job that I was obliged to turn it down. She replied with grace and kindness to my letter, wishing me well and hoping that a future opportunity might see me able to return. I have kept that letter; I appreciated the fact that she took the time to write it. Ben never went to a childminder again. I have never held a career post since.

PART 2

Meeting the World

CHAPTER 9

The First School

I tried to start planning early for the move to school. The plans for The Statement were under way and I visited several schools, including one with provision for children with speech problems. This unit was interesting but as we were unclear about the exact nature of Ben's difficulties, it was concluded that this might not be suitable.

I visited our local catchment school several times: I believed it was the best way to remove some of the fear from the first few days. It was unfamiliar to both of us as the local catchment areas had been changed since his brothers attended primary school. The office staff already seemed to have formed the opinion that I was a fussy, over-protective mother. They later told me that my son had greater learning difficulties than they had ever handled before. This was a learning curve for them also.

The school was a twenty-minute walk from my home and my first thought was how I could entice him to get there without a pushchair or a car. I decided we would take a bus for two stops to reduce the walking needed and to introduce a bit of adventure and fun into the journey. It was a struggle. He gradually grew accustomed to it. I was grateful in those early days for the occasional lift from another mum who lived on the way to the bus stop. I was unsure in the beginning if he could even be persuaded to wear the school uniform but after the initial few days, he accepted this. I was relieved.

The first few months of school passed in a blur. He looked so small and frightened as I handed him over each morning. He rarely spoke outside of the family, didn't read, count or understand much of what was going on around him. He did not engage in play with other children. He loved looking out of the window watching the birds, flapping his hands. He had his own support worker for part of the school day, courtesy of his Statement, the Magic Key to accessing help. Soon after his arrival, the school applied for additional hours and from then on, he had support for almost all of his school day.

He still had frequent toileting accidents and I was summoned to the school to discuss the issue as he could not cope without adult help. At first I was told that I might have to go to the school each time this occurred and Ben might have to go home every lunch time as his assistants were not expected to carry out personal care. I could see my newly-acquired free time disappearing before my eyes. I would not be able to work, to get jobs done at home or to relax. There would be a lot of walking to and fro. Fortunately help came in the form of one kind teaching assistant who offered to undertake these duties. It was not part of her job and there was no financial incentive for her. She had offered to do this unpleasant job just because she wanted to help Ben and me. I was so grateful to her for this humanitarian gesture. Her kindness afforded me those chinks of freedom, a few hours when I could live my own life again. It made such a difference to me at this time.

The parents in the playground were mostly kind and engaging. In the early years, my son was invited to parties as a member of the small class or as a result of my friendship with the other mums. Later these invitations tailed off as the children developed their closer circles of friends.

The school always included everyone in their Harvest, Christmas and class assemblies and I was very proud of the one line he was once given to read on one of these occasions.

Whilst he was attending this school, a breakfast club was set up. The children came out of school in a flurry of excitement with their fliers inviting everyone to think of starting their day having breakfast and chilling out at the new facility. My son went a couple of times, just to try it out. He did not go for the full time offered; in fact, he was only there for twenty to thirty minutes. He did not misbehave and he loved it! Soon after this, I was asked not to send him anymore as 'adequate supervision for him could not be provided'. I wrote to the head teacher expressing my regret and my doubts whether his request complied with current disability legislation. He replied that as this was not part of the official school day, that law did not apply. The tone of the letter expressed displeasure. I was not totally sure of the school's legal stance but aware that I needed the school's support both for the present and to forge my son's future. Sometimes, pragmatism has to prevail. I did not pursue the legal issue. He never went to breakfast club again, though I know his support worker was willing to supervise him there sometimes, if required.

On sports day, all children took part in a series of games and activities, culminating in a series of running races with their peers. Ben was a good runner but took his starting cue from the runners next to him rather than the signal given. This meant he always started several seconds after them. After a few years of watching these races, I positioned myself at the finish line and began to give him my own order to start. He eventually came away with a sports day medal.

In his final year at junior school, a teacher introduced cross country running. Ben was quite good at this, as long as he did not become distracted along the route. I often wondered if some of the other boys deliberately did so to slow his progress as they competed for positions. On one occasion, I actually heard another child give him misleading instructions. As they well knew, Ben always did what they told him to! Eventually, the school team was chosen for the first event and Ben did not make the cut. However, for the next one, his name was on the list and we were given an invitation slip for him to represent the school. Unfortunately, our elation was short-lived as it was later rescinded. Someone had misread the number of participants required. The disappointment was chilling. Finally, he did represent the school at cross country and as his proud mother I watched the race with eager encouragement for him as he passed. It was a proud day!

Some of the other children became less understanding as they progressed through the school and taunted and tricked him. One day they told him to tip up the playground bin. For them, it was a prank. For him it was an instruction from 'friends'. He never thought to refuse. He had been told to do something, so he did it. In reality, it was a power game, an act of bullying, a cruel incident. As the bin clattered over, spilling its contents, the other boys disappeared, laughing loudly. Ben was left to take the consequences. I was summoned to the Headmaster's study. Ben was confused and distressed. The head teacher felt that he must not make Ben an exception to the school rules, though he recognised that Ben did not understand the implications of his action. In fact, his only sanction was to discuss the issue with us, punishment enough for Ben who found this disturbing. I expressed my desire for the bullies to be called to account though I do not know if this ever happened.

Years later, I witnessed one of these boys mocking my son on several occasions at school and club sporting events. His attitude had not changed. He was a bright child, a high achiever, probably destined for a top university and a job in the city. I walked away again with a mixture of disgust and pity.

My son had several great teachers at his Primary school but his life was perhaps more profoundly affected by the diligence, care and personal engagement of his learning support assistants. These were the individuals who steered his education on a daily basis, who recognised and rejoiced over his incremental progress and who helped to construct his fragile self-esteem. Many of these cared deeply for him. One always stops me when I meet her, eager to catch up on his news, despite her professional engagement having ended a decade ago. These are the unsung heroes of the educational system and we remain forever in their debt.

CHAPTER 10

Learning to Play Football

Prejudice is not a tick box yes or no, it is a something we all have in some measure; a continuum. Some are further along the scale than others but in a continuum we are all there somewhere. Prejudice is normally directed towards minority or disadvantaged groups: ginger-haired, ethnic minorities, acne-faced, disabled, low-income families. It may be linked with the instinct of survival of the fittest but it has its origins in insecurity, power and control.

I was one day given a leaflet about an after-school sports club run at a local special school. I don't know whether I was not yet ready to admit my son's level of need but I chose to dismiss this. My child, though struggling was at a mainstream school after all!

Soon afterwards all the children came out of school one day with great excitement, waving coloured flyers. The local football team was offering to run an after-school club, open to all. Most of the boys were desperate to join and my son was no exception. We duly returned the form, paid the fee and on the first day, the boys were there decked in their school PE kit, ready to become the next Wayne Rooney. The coach who arrived with his club emblem emblazoned on every piece of kit was far removed from the sporting hunk we parents expected. He was of average build, wiry rather than athletic and walked with a stoop, suggestive of some permanent dysfunction. I informed him of my son's difficulties and he nodded, without listening. The invitation clearly implied the sessions were open to all. As I watched with the other mums I became more and more concerned. He had little rapport with any children and limited ideas of football drills.

At the end of the third week, he approached me, with Ben.

"Are you his parent?"

"Yes, I replied," totally unprepared for what was to follow.

"He doesn't listen or follow my instructions. *I don't want him to come any more.*"

This lightning bolt was so unfair, so unexpected that it left me staggering on the inside, shocked. There was no discussion, no questions just summary dismissal. I said nothing; my only retaliation was a hard, icy stare. I deliberately sustained eye contact for a lengthy moment, enough I hoped to express my pain, disgust and disbelief. The coach said nothing and emotionlessly walked away.

One of the bystanders, who knew Ben well, turned to me.

"Are you OK? You aren't going to just accept that, are you? That's discrimination. You should complain. He can't do that! You should make a formal complaint."

"Yes, I know." I said, but at that moment I just needed to escape.

Sometimes you are so hurt that you have to walk away. I know I should have done all of those things and would have done so on another occasion but this was one of those moments when the flame was beyond yellow and red. The pain was white hot and I had to choose flight. I would fight many other battles but today I had no fighting strength.

How do you tell a child that he is not welcome because of things beyond his control?

"Don't worry! Mummy will find you some better football training." I assured him as I grasped his hand and we wearily walked away.

Within days, I took my son to the football training at the special needs school. Instantly, I knew I had made the right decision. The people running it were welcoming, inclusive, friendly, with a genuine love of children and an outstanding commitment to helping them enjoy sport whatever their level of ability. He went to many sports sessions and holiday activity days there, learning basic skills in trampolining, basketball, dodgeball and swimming as well as football. The staff there helped him to understand some of the football rules that he had struggled to grasp - in particular the need to shoot at one end of a football pitch instead of both, which had proved frustrating for children playing with him. They reinforced the social skills of turn-taking and team play, with charm and grace, mixed with much fun, in an atmosphere without judgement. This boosted his self-esteem and taught him skills which have opened up a social world to him.

Whilst my son's ability to socialise increased, my prejudices decreased, and I found in the other parents there kindred spirits and true understanding. I also saw the courage of parents and teachers coping with greater problems than my own. Thank you all for the inspiration you were to us - you changed our lives!

CHAPTER 11

The First Trophy

My son, unlike his siblings had few certificates and trophies when he was young. No swimming badges because we abandoned formal classes. No spelling or maths test certificates. Not even full attendance as he always had a few hospital appointments to drop him just short of the required total. He only ever received the occasional encouragement certificate that every child had through the year, awarded towards the end of the school year, when someone checked. It is easy for teachers to forget how much effort is required to make the smallest advance for the weaker pupils, especially when disability and disappointment come together and progress is incremental, at best, so the first time my son was given a trophy was very special.

We had been attending the disability football classes for a few weeks. At the end of the session the children were sitting expectantly for the announcement, when my son was called out to receive his honours. His face lit up with pride and pleasure as he stepped forward to take hold of the award, a football figure standing about six inches high, a bronze colour with a crest on the base - his to keep for a week, along with the smile that accompanied it!

At home, we responded to this event with great ceremony. We phoned the grandparents, took photographs, told friends and made the trophy the focal point of our lounge, giving it centre stage on our sparsely populated mantelpiece. So many times, he had watched as his brothers had brought home medals, trophies and certificates - now this was his moment of triumph. This was not just a piece of moulded resin, sprayed to bronze, it was a milestone!

For four days, it commanded respect and admiration from its elevated vantage point. On the fifth day, the unthinkable happened. I do not know how. I only know that one minute it was staring at me majestically from its dignified position. The next, I was gazing at a myriad of shattered pieces on the floor, filled with a mixture of panic and disbelief. How could I have let this happen? How could I tell him - or the football class? What would they think of me? I was filled with a profound disgust as I berated my carelessness and my folly; that momentary sense of disbelief and despair that makes you feel physically ill before eventually expressing itself in silent screams and waterless tears. After a few minutes of internal rage and self-flagellation, the raw emotion gave way to logical thought. What could I do?

A first glance at the pile of pieces made me think the best option would be to purchase a replacement. By way of last resort, however, I carefully gathered every last shard, just in case, and stored them in a safe place.

There were two shops in town that supplied the local sports clubs and schools with trophies, so I changed my plans for the day and set off on my new mission. At the first, I surveyed the window then asked inside, but without success. As I approached the second, I was aware that my quest had become more urgent. A first glance revealed no matches so I went inside and explained my predicament. The shopkeeper informed me that the styles of these trophies changed regularly so the one in question had probably been purchased before the current styles had been issued. He showed me a variety of similar products at various prices. There was no exact match to be had. I now had a new dilemma. If I bought a new trophy, I would have to confess my crime not just to my son but to the group as well. It was not a cheap option either financially of in terms of my hurt pride! I told the shopkeeper I would go away and think about it and returned to assess the viability of plan B.

I spent the next two and a half days piecing together my 3D puzzle with a tube of superglue and a great deal of determination. It had to be possible! It had to be perfect! The members of my household were sceptical but increasingly fascinated as my project took shape.

By the time my son was ready to return to the football class, it looked good; it looked very good - most importantly it did not look like it was held together by superglue! I did not try to pretend that nothing had happened, though I think I could have pulled it off. I did not either paint a detailed picture of what had happened or my frantic few days trying to put it right.

"I am afraid I dropped it but have managed to glue it back together with superglue," I said tentatively.

"Oh, don't worry - it wouldn't have been the first time. We have had to replace it several times!"

Undecided whether to mourn my lost time or admire my handiwork, I smiled politely and relaxed for the first time in three days!

CHAPTER 12

Table Tennis

A large chunk of our living room is taken up by a table tennis table. It is three-quarter size, the usual bottle green with white markings and cost less than one hundred pounds in a sale a few weeks before Christmas. They only had two left in the shop and unusually I made a snap decision to buy it as a combined present for our three sons, before wondering how I would get it home! It was an impulse buy, fuelled by nostalgia; of my own happy memories of playing mainly in the garden on a table lovingly fashioned by my father, a carpenter by trade.

What a bargain! We too have spent many hours locked in fiercely competitive family tournaments or playing as a backdrop to serious decision-making. For Ben, table tennis has become a tool for social acceptance - one of the few arenas where he can positively stand out from the crowd - and a calming agent. Our wallpaper also bears a permanent indent, a sober reminder of the night he threw a table tennis bat in anger, inches from my head.

For Ben, it began when his junior school accepted an offer from a local coach to give introductory lessons to their pupils. Using fun approaches with gadgets and games, he initiated a generation of pupils to the sport of table tennis. Behind the fun and jokes, he taught them proper techniques and a number began to develop decent skills. He came to the school fete that year, running both fun sessions and a tournament. It was one of the highlights of the event and one of the last activities to be cleared away. This coach didn't just teach; he inspired! When he finished his last session at the school, he gave out fliers advertising the local club he ran, with an award of a free introductory session to a handful of pupils who showed potential. Amongst that limited group were two children with special educational needs. Ben went along with his special invitation and loved it; he received regular coaching, played tournaments, met new people, was accepted, fitted in.

Unfortunately, the original coach left after a year or so, taking up an international coaching appointment. He was adored by the youngsters and we attended an emotional send-off at a bowling alley where we had gathered for a chance to relax together and say goodbye. The coach cried and most of the young people and parents shed tears also. Ben was sorry to see him leave but confused at this display of emotion that he did not understand.

This coach was replaced by his antithesis, another serious stroke technician, with excellent knowledge of the game but considerably less rapport with his students. The first night as I watched him and my son, I thought this would never work. My son was at times interrupting his lengthy explanations and struggling to concentrate or follow his complex instructions. The coach appeared irritated, sullen.

"Do I try and explain things to this coach or do we go quietly before we are asked to leave?"

I could see only one outcome. I discussed it with the club secretary, a mother but also a teaching assistant at my son's school, who knew him well and shared my fears that this new relationship would not work.

"Don't leave yet," she said. "Let me have a word, let me see what I can do."

This was a kind lady, who was proud of the club's record on inclusivity but aware of the privilege of acquiring a top-level coach and the difficulty of marrying these two ideas. I do not know what she said or did. I only know that both my son and the coach mellowed in their approach; working, perhaps unconsciously, at 'making it happen'. It could be that my son interrupted less or the explanations were shortened, but between them, they managed to accommodate each other.

My son's ability to play increased. We continued attending the club regularly until the club folded for financial reasons. Ben has never stopped enjoying table tennis and has played for his school, reaching a National Final event. He was awarded school colours in table tennis and twice won a Gold Medal at a local Disability Sports Event. The table tennis table was indeed a bargain; the social currency gained, inestimable!

CHAPTER 13

The Storm and the Rainbow

At the end of each school year, as any parent knows, there is a day when the teaching groups are announced for the following year. It is anticipated with mixed emotions by parents and pupils. There is always a special buzz in the playground that day and a lively post-mortem the day afterwards. If you know the staff involved, you may react accordingly, though class decisions are never changed by complaining children or prejudiced parents. First-time parents are keen to evaluate the gossip from parents with older siblings or inside information. Children are keen to know their fate from older children in the school.

On this occasion, I knew little about the name on Ben's slip. I recognised the teacher as young, with long dark hair. I knew little else. My son had no more information so we opted to assume the best and await the return to school in September.

At the end of the first day back, this teacher asked to see me. She had not had a good day! She informed me that Ben had not made a good impression. *He did not listen to instructions, he did not ... he could not... his behaviour was not acceptable.* She had clearly marked his card as difficult, a problem. Ben was agitated and upset. This was not a good start to the school year!

Within a few weeks, it became apparent that her problems were wider than my son. The teacher resigned and left and crisis measures were put in place until a permanent replacement could be found. Part of these crisis measures included placing Ben with a class of children in the year below. It was presented to him as a special job for him to help and encourage the younger children. He was the only one. I voiced my concerns but could do little but accept this as a temporary measure. After a couple of weeks, this pretence was wearing thin. Ben was questioning why he was being treated differently; so was I. I spoke to the head teacher, who asked me for a little more time, assuring me he had plans afoot which would be highly beneficial for my son.

He was as good as his word. Shortly afterwards, 'The Rainbow Room' was born. What the head teacher had done was set up a mini resource base for the some of the neediest children in the school to receive their education in a small group separate from their peers made up of pupils of mixed ages but similar needs. It was run initially by teaching assistants, supported by the SENCO, following a simpler version of the curriculum with many practical, hands-on tasks. My son loved this group and the cooking, modelling and painting that were embraced as media for learning. He spent the remaining time at Primary school based in this unit. It had an intimate atmosphere and he always took a birthday cake into class to share with his group. Perhaps it was here for the first time, he felt accepted. It was indeed the rainbow offering hope after the battering of the storm.

CHAPTER 14

The Adventure Holiday

There was a ripple of excitement as the children emerged from school that day, gradually echoed by the mums as the news spread. The much-awaited letters about the school holiday had been distributed to my son's year group. The letter outlined details of the five-day holiday at an outdoor activity centre several hours' drive away. Accommodation was in huts and the children would be engaged in a variety of fun, challenging and exhausting games and activities. The children were enthusiastically discussing what they would and would not do when they got there. The invitation was to all the pupils in the year group. Ben, as always wanted to be like everyone else, though the implications of what was involved did not register in his mind as they were outside of his current experience. For most of the children it would be the first time away from home. Secretly, many had a few fears mixed in with their excitement but amongst the boys, at least, it was not admitted in the playground. They were too cool to be that honest!

For Ben to engage in this adventure, he would need the additional support he received every day at school. Shortly after receiving the letter, I spoke to the school about whether this could be arranged. I was politely asked to leave it with them and they would see what could be done. At intervals over the next few months, I approached the school asking for their response. Every time, procrastination was the order of the day. At one point, one of his teaching assistants had been willing to go on the trip and support him. Later, her own circumstances changed and this was no longer possible.

Eventually, I found myself in the head teacher's study a few weeks before the trip, asking the same question. He apologised, said the issue had been forgotten and Ben could go on the trip if we could escort him. Neither Richard nor I could go on this trip as we both had to be at work. He suggested one of our older sons could take our place. This seemed unfair but was anyway not possible. Finally, he cheerily suggested that we could nominate anyone else provided they had a current, valid CRB check. I do not know whether the issue had been left deliberately or by mistake or simply because no-one knew what to do. I only know that to me at that time this seemed like the ultimate killer move in a mind game. I knew no-one available at such short notice in possession of the necessary documentation. We both knew that obtaining a new CRB check for anyone in that time was impossible. Game over!

I stared hard, deeply into his eyes. It was a gesture of despair, of a sense of betrayal, of a feeling of being stitched-up but ultimately a sense of helplessness.

Ben joined the few pupils left for a week of games and activities at school, organised by a kind teacher who tried his best to convince this remnant that they were not settling for second best. He failed, inevitably, but he did give them fun and a good time. I never did succeed in answering my son's question:

"Why couldn't I go on the Adventure Holiday with my class?"

In my mind, defeat and despair were soon followed by a determination to make up for my son's loss. However, with limited resources and two other children to look after, my options were limited. As I recounted these events to a neighbour, herself a mother of two disabled youngsters, she told me about a charity set up to make wishes come true for seriously sick and disabled children. She recounted how they had funded most of her family's recent trip to Disneyland Paris and suggested we ask for a similar wish.

My first thought was that Ben was not needy enough. He was not seriously ill and not as severely disabled as her children. She said they had recently broadened their criteria anyway and suggested I write to them. In my letter, I explained what had happened with the school holiday. I explained my son's level of disability and awaited their response. A few weeks later, I received a call from a kind lady informing me that they would like to grant my son's wish to go to Disneyland Paris for a weekend. I could barely speak, I felt so humbled, so grateful, my belief in humanity instantly restored. She discussed dates, needs and preferences. They paid for Ben and an escort. We paid for an extra adult and the three of us went on an exciting adventure.

For Ben, it was the holiday of a lifetime. I know there were occasional moments of tension but I have chosen to block them from my memory. What remains is an idyllic holiday, where we could give our son all our attention, freed from the responsibilities of work, other siblings and other pressures. We had two day passes so were able to visit both Disney parks. We obtained a special disability pass which meant we did not have to queue for long periods. This was vital to the success of the holiday as it avoided the danger of public outbursts resulting from anxiety or frustration. Autistic children struggle greatly with long waits and public arenas like this offer nowhere to hide if the worst should happen.

We went on every ride we chose, saw everything we wanted and stayed at a Disney-themed hotel on the outskirts of the Disney Resort, where even the soap was shaped like Mickey Mouse! We went to a Cowboy evening, complete with cattle-rounding displays, where we all dressed in cowboy hats and ate chunks of beef off wooden slabs. We were still enjoying our final ride twenty minutes before the Eurostar left and we collapsed, exhausted but exhilarated into our reserved seats. I can never thank those strangers enough for what they did for us at a real low point. I think Ben's special holiday memories will outlive those of his school peers. The picture montage we made of the trip has been a focal point in his bedroom ever since.

PART 3

At Secondary School

CHAPTER 15

The Transition

We began early looking at possible schools for Ben to continue his education. Our best-fit was a special needs school in the neighbouring borough. This school was popular, with long waiting lists. The school was small, the layout straightforward. My son knew many students in different classes through his football club so he would already have friends there. We applied twice and were refused. The first time we accepted the decision.

During the second application process a year later, the head teacher admitted that he would be willing to offer him a place if one was available. This implied that my son did meet the criteria for this placement. However, to receive it, we needed the agreement of the LEA which was refused. We appealed and they refused again. The only course remaining was to request a tribunal hearing; taking our case to a third party. It took me nearly eight months to prepare our case, gathering information, collating evidence, formulating a defence of our request. It became my unpaid employment, a research project more like a thesis.

We were given a deadline for our submission and a date for the hearing. We remained optimistic until we received notification of the LEA's defence including their estimate of the costs which included transport provided to and from our home for five years. I gasped as I read the figures presented. I felt that had I requisitioned a limousine and paid a chauffeur, I could not have arrived at such an elevated figure. I also found out that a minibus already travelled a similar route, paid for by our LEA. It had spaces on board.

We had already looked long and hard at the other options. There were three: a specialist autism school; a special needs school for students with a wide range of learning difficulties and a large secondary school which housed a unit for students with additional needs from all over the borough.

The first, which I visited on several occasions, would not offer him a place as they required a diagnosis of moderate to severe autism which we did not have.

The second had evident measures in place for dealing with challenging behaviour including restricted access to rooms and corridors. I also witnessed a major incident during my visit which left me shocked. Despite the kindness of the staff here, I did not feel my son required this provision.

The third option was the comprehensive school at the other side of town. It was more than twice the size of his previous school. Ben did not know any of the students or staff. It was in an area we never frequented, nearly half an hour's car journey from our home. I visited the school on several occasions. The staff were pleasant, the SENCO sympathetic. They would have a place for him in the Unit. We might be eligible for transport from the LEA. It was our decision.

We tried one last time to secure our first-choice school. We arranged a meeting to discuss our case with a representative of the LEA. Richard and I decided to offer to transport our child ourselves thus greatly reducing the costs, if they would agree to the placement. It was an offer to meet halfway; Ben would have the school place we felt was best suited to him but without such an elevated cost to the taxpayer. They declined our offer. Then as we were about to leave, she delivered the cruellest of blows informing us that if we proceeded with the Tribunal and lost, the LEA would determine the school for our child. Our second choice would not be held open. Not even for two weeks, despite the offer from the school to do so. Wounded, angry, disbelieving, we stumbled out of the large chamber in our local council building into the sunlight of a summer day outside.

"I feel like we've been blackmailed", whispered Richard, in disbelief. I did not disagree.

There was nothing more to be done. Realising we had tried and failed, we chose to withdraw our case and pursue our second choice with enthusiasm and diligence, which is where we went next.

Once the comprehensive school was informed, staff began to make arrangements for visits and communicate with us and his primary school but time was limited as this was well into the summer term. We visited this school several times. With around sixteen hundred pupils, it was vast. It contained a small unit where most of my son's classes would be held but he remained part of the wider school community and attended some lessons in different rooms scattered around the site.

It was adjoining a large council estate, as far in the opposite direction from our home as the school of our choice. The only concession we secured was the guarantee of transport provided for at least three years - no promises were made for the last two. The transport arranged for him consisted of a minibus collecting a number of pupils on a journey across town that took forty-five minutes. He had to be ready at seven-thirty in the morning as he was one of the first pupils collected by an unfamiliar driver and escort.

It was no surprise that Ben found the first weeks frightening, bewildering, confusing and difficult. He knew no-one. There was little we could do to cushion the shock. I wondered if the administrator who had made the decision ever thought to compare the figures for the similar journeys in different directions or realised the human cost. I reflected how easy it must be to make decisions and sign documents in an office far removed from the families affected by them, in a place where names and places are typescript code, divorced from human form, void of emotion.

CHAPTER 16

The Exclusion

Ben had barely crossed the threshold of his new school when I was kindly informed that they wished to help him to become more independent and were therefore keen to 'wean him off the high level of support' he had received at his junior school. Whilst this sounded praiseworthy, I already felt uneasy about the whole thing. There was after all a reason why that support had been put in place and this time of already great change did not seem the moment to bring more disruption to the status quo. However, they were the professionals, I thought, though I also wondered if they had read the many notes of acquired wisdom that accompanied my son on his arrival, from their junior school colleagues.

After a few days, it was already clear that the staff were beginning to change their viewpoint. I had a conversation with the SENCO who promised to set up a supervised place of safety for my son during breaks and lunchtimes as he was not coping with the unstructured times. Initially this meant that he could go to a small room in a staff area with one or two pupils where they could chill out away from the hurly-burly of the vast school field and the frenetic activity of the playground. She hoped in time to be able to re-establish a larger, more organised lunch time club which had once run for vulnerable pupils but had been disbanded.

Four long weeks passed and despite her efforts, the lunch club remained an item somewhere on people's agenda. The issue had been raised, passed on to another layer of bureaucracy, required the agreement of this individual, that team, this finance… then one day changed everything.

As my son returned from school, it was immediately evident that he was very agitated.

"I'm sorry! I didn't mean to do it," he blurted.

I knew from his malaise that something big was up.

"A letter, there's a letter in my bag. You must read it!"

I pulled the letter from his bag, unprepared for what it contained.

Dear Parent

Your son/daughter will be excluded from all lessons tomorrow because of assaulting another pupil. Please send him/her to Room 12 to be supervised by the Head of Year.

Please sign and return the slip below.

Signed…………………………………………… Head of Year

Inside, my sense of horror and of shame was overwhelming, but this would have to wait.

"What happened?"

"I hit a girl in my class. I didn't mean to. It wasn't my fault..."

"What did she do? Why did you do it?"

I remember no more about that day except the sense of family honour destroyed and the necessity to calm the distressed child in front of me, something I was unqualified to do. I called Richard. He was always better able to bring calm. After Ben finally fell asleep, exhausted, we discussed the day's events but though much was felt, little was said. Sometimes there is no formal vocabulary to express what exists in your head!

The following morning, Ben was too volatile to go to school by his usual minibus so I waved it past and took him to school by car.

I went with him to the school entrance and after he had entered, I went to the reception and requested an appointment with the head teacher.

"I'm sorry that is not possible today."

"That's fine," I understand," I will see one of the deputy head teachers... any of the senior management...SENCO..."

"They are also unavailable. There is no-one who can see you today. The earliest appointment to see the head teacher is in two days' time. Would you like to see the Headmaster at 10 am on Thursday?"

I looked through the locked doors to the corridors and classrooms bustling with school life. So many people, no-one available. Disbelief!

"Sorry, you are telling me that no-one in a position of authority in this school will see me today?" I began to explain a little of the seriousness behind my sudden request and how I had driven twenty-five minutes just to see someone here in person. The receptionist was unflinching. My comments did not appear to register in her mind.

As I left, I asked her to take to the head teacher a signed written statement that I expected the school to take full responsibility for any further violent conduct by my son occurring that day including any harm to other pupils or staff since I had come to discuss matters with the school and been refused. She took the piece of paper from me and nodded her assent.

I walked out of the school building slowly to my car, sat behind the steering wheel, my head in my hands and wept tears of frustration and despair. After some time had passed, I phoned a friend, still crying and told her what had happened. She drove over to see me and shared my anguish until I was composed enough to drive home.

Two days later, the head teacher apologised for the distress caused but explained this was the school's normal procedure. Perhaps, I suggested, extraordinary events required modification of this procedure. I think he half agreed but I remained unconvinced that the practice would be changed. He was however, very supportive and began to discuss a range of measures that would help Ben to settle and avoid such crises. He said he would immediately implement the measures proposed four weeks earlier; a lunchtime club with structured activities and adult supervision was to be set up.

I had to be grateful. We had to look forward; *you cannot change the past*! My son and many other vulnerable individuals were to be spared the daily barrage of bullying and bewilderment which the unstructured times of the school day offered. Progress. Just tinged with pity that if they had acted on recommendations carefully prepared by the junior school or had their own proposals not tarried in their bureaucratic system, we need never have reached this point. We could not look back; *you can change the future!*

CHAPTER 17

The Iced Bun and the Policeman

Ben had barely been at his new school a matter of days when I received a phone call informing me that he had been caught stealing from the school canteen. The school regarded this as a serious matter and wished to invite a policeman to talk to my son to underline the seriousness of the incident. Instantly, my mind was flooded with a video clip of my son, probably unaware of what he had done, certainly unaware of the seriousness of his crime, being read his rights before being questioned by a stern, uniformed policeman, a blot next to his name, if not a criminal record. My video clip moved on to him, older now, living a life of crime in a social underworld, doing the bidding of manipulative figures taking advantage of his ignorance and willingness to obey orders. He was a helpless, lost soul, being sentenced to jail for his criminal activities, carried away to an unknown world of incarceration and exploitation...

"You are aware that my son has special needs," I said, re-emerging from my reverie with an urgent sense of purpose, "that he had no money on him, that he has never been in a shop or a café without an adult, that he does not understand how to use money…"

As I listened to myself, I realised I was sounding more and more like a mother making excuses, out of touch with reality, attempting to defend the indefensible. I alone knew that was not the case. I was aware most teachers would see things differently.

"Perhaps you could explain precisely what happened?"

"He was in the canteen with a couple of the boys from his class who each bought an iced bun. He took a bun from the rack and proceeded to eat it in front of everyone, without making any attempt to pay for it. Inevitably, the other children watching called him a thief, the dinner ladies spoke to him and the duty teachers were called. We take stealing very seriously at this school."

"Of course you do, so do I, but this is no ordinary case," I thought silently in the intervening pause.

"My child has a Statement, so I would like the SENCO to be involved in deciding how to proceed and I would like to speak to her before any action is taken, please."

The matter was decided with due consideration for my son's learning difficulties, including his limited understanding of basic concepts, inability to handle money and his state of total confusion at starting at a large secondary school, several miles from home. He was given a disciplinary sanction and told the school's view on taking things that do not belong to you. He was not allowed in the canteen without an adult escort and it was explained to him that if he wished to have something from the canteen, he would have to bring some money and pay the dinner lady before he could eat it.

"No money means no eating canteen food."

He took dinner money for a few days and was guided through the process of buying food with an adult helper. The novelty soon wore off and he asked to resume his packed lunches. He never took food from the canteen again.

I cannot remember whether the community policeman was drafted in but if so, it was more of a chat than an interrogation, an explanation than a rebuke. However, haunted by my vision, it would be a long time before I let him go to any shop or café again unescorted. The long process of learning to handle money had begun its progress in incremental steps, at a pace so slow as to be almost invisible to the observing eye. I chose to believe what I could not see, that progress was being made, at least until proven otherwise.

CHAPTER 18

The Diagnosis at Last

"You *must* get a formal diagnosis for us to get the help that your son needs."

These words from the SENCO at my son's secondary school, weeks after his arrival left no doubt. In the end, we pursued the quest for a diagnosis with urgency and persistence. So far from the day that the word autism had first been shot so brutally by the speech therapist at our lives, we were the ones in fierce pursuit of the big label. It would not be obtained without effort.

When you have waited for something for a long time, the last part of the waiting game seems to be the slowest of all. Now, after all that had happened, we had decided it was time: we were ready; we wanted action. The other players in this game were not so motivated. They were bound by a system of slow-moving bureaucracy. A referral here. A waiting list there. An appointment system for this clinic. The long-awaited consultation.

We came with an air of determination and business manner in no mood to back down until we had secured our deal. We had arrived armed with a series of video recordings as irrefutable evidence of verbal and physical menace, testament to the issues we faced daily as a family and the aberrant behaviours we witnessed as part of our everyday family life. We were shown into a large room with a conference table and without delay, we delivered our lecture. The grey-haired lady watched in silent obedience with a deepening look of shock on her face. By the end of our performance, she looked in need of support herself. She weakly commented that she now understood the difficulties that we were facing but explained that she was not qualified to make a diagnosis. She was in fact a holding administrator, whose role was never made clear to us, with authority only to wave us on to the next level. We briefly vented our frustration, somewhat unfairly, on this individual but she was the only person to represent the great wall of bureaucracy and we were not willing to slink quietly away.

Eventually the final appointment came but by this time all our emotion was spent. We repeated the film show but with the desperation this time replaced by resignation and a tinge of despair. The consultant was purposeful and business-like with a hint of kindness in her eyes. Her verdict: mild autism with learning difficulties.

I felt nothing on an emotional level, after all, I told myself, 'nothing has changed'. My only response was the business-like thought that we might fare better without the word 'mild' on the document. Rights and responsibilities were often fiercely disputed over minor words! How callous, I thought to myself - what have I become?

When we arrived home, we exhaled deeply, a sense of having

reached a goal exhausted after a great deal of effort. We had achieved our aim. The long quest was over. It was not long before we realised that this was not the end at all, simply a milestone on a much longer quest, one which would last beyond our lifetime. The real aim was to prepare our son for the highest quality of life that he could enjoy, far beyond the present into his old age. We had barely begun!

CHAPTER 19

The Birthday Party

Birthday parties are events that as a child we look forward to with great anticipation for a long time. However good they are, they seem almost doomed to fall short. As a parent, you try your best to make everything go smoothly. With hindsight, I could have made a different choice on this occasion at a key point which might have induced a different outcome. Hindsight, however, was unavailable to me at the time.

Ben was to have a birthday party at a local bowling alley. There were to be six in total, four boys from his school, as well as one he had known from his junior school and Ben. As we lived the other side of town, I picked up four boys from school that day. There was much chatter between them as I drove the twenty-five-minute journey home. Ben was excited but so too were the other boys, some of whom rarely ventured out for such social events. We stopped at home briefly for the boys to change out of their school clothes into casual gear. The friends were fascinated with the novelty of our house and its contents and thrilled to meet Ben's older brothers. He opened his cards and gifts with much excitement and genuine pleasure as the others helped with the unpacking and looked on eagerly. Everything was going to plan for a perfect day!

We arrived at the venue where we were joined by the other two boys, including one whose mother had travelled by bus with him and decided to stay until they went home. The boys noisily explored the venue, including trying buttons and handles on the various games machines that fringed the bowling lanes.

"No, I'm sorry I can't give you money for the machine games but after the bowling, you can have a few goes at either pool or air hockey."

The boys were grateful and accepting and after a few wistful attempts to make the gaming machines work without coins, they joined us in trying to kit each one out with an appropriate sized pair of bowling shoes. Few seemed to have a clear idea of their size and several needed help with tying the laces but the job was soon done and the boys were ready. They played on two adjacent alleys – one with a rest to guide the balls and one without. The bowling began. What I had forgotten was that boys of this age are fiercely competitive and hate losing. Ben was no exception. I had also forgotten that though he enjoyed bowling, he was not particularly good at it. I had steered him towards the rest and he was scoring some points but not the strikes and spares of some of his friends. I guess the tension had begun to build...

I had bought a jug of drink for each table so that the boys would not get thirsty. A few of the boys asked for coke or lemonade but accepted the squash drink I had placed on the table without further question. Then Ben began to perseverate... He wanted coke. All his friends wanted coke. It was his birthday... We were mean, horrible... he *had* to have coke. At first, we tried to brush it off with logical argument. We had already bought the squash. His friends had accepted it; they were not upset. Perhaps he could have lemonade another day... My parent/teacher instinct was telling me that we had said no so we should stick with our decision. A short time later, I would have bought every can of coke in the place just to escape. By then, it would have made no difference.

My memories of that day are like being sucked into the vortex of a tornado, with Ben shouting obscenities at Richard and me at the top of his voice, declaring how unkind we were, haranguing us with threats and language associated with a street brawl in an inner city late on a Saturday night and all with his friends and some of their parents looking on with a mixture of disappointment, disgust and disbelief as the party disintegrated around us. I remember some of the friends trying to calm him down, talking to him, trying to help. I remember some of them being distressed at the loss of control, the words uttered unjustly at us parents and the underlying sadness of seeing their friend's special day go so horribly wrong. My other sons were in the melee trying alternately to calm him down and redeem something for the other boys, playing pool and air hockey, distracting them from something we were powerless to change.

I talked to the other parents, apologised, tried to act as if the unfolding chaos was not really happening, wishing to be able to turn back the clock, give them cokes, enjoy the event... Inside I felt humiliated, exposed, judged and alone. For the first time for many years our son's issues had spilled out into a public theatre, an impromptu performance of his worst talents played before an audience of his carefully nurtured friends and their caring, protecting parents. I doubted if any there would ever accept him as a friend again.

After that day, the mother who had witnessed the whole event never allowed her son to meet mine outside of school, except for later birthday parties where she accompanied him. He never came to our house again and my son has never been invited to his. At school and supervised holiday activities, they remained good friends. Of the remainder, one proved a particularly loyal friend and supporter at school and visited our house whenever we could arrange it. Another visited occasionally. I do not blame anyone who refused contact after that event. I am amazed at the ability of young people to forgive, accept, support and befriend.

CHAPTER 20

Climbing His Mountain (Live on The Big Stage)

When Ben was young, I sometimes took him to see a pantomime or a children's play in our local theatre. Always, as he pointed to the stage, he would say:

"I want to do that. I want to go up there!"

Like most parents, I replied without much thought.

"Perhaps one day when you are bigger."

As the years went by and we became more aware of his difficulties, my answers sounded more and more hollow as my mind dismissed the possibility.

Several years later, I came across an advert for a drama workshop for children with special needs. I spoke to Ben and his face lit up. His dream began to take shape but there were still several peaks to climb for this mountain to be conquered!

....

When he noticed the advert in the weekly newsletter for the school musical, my son was keen to go. We booked our tickets and arrived on a snowy December evening, just in time for the performance. At the interval, as we moved to the school canteen for drinks and snacks, he looked straight into my eyes:

"Next year, I want to be in it!"

As we left that night, we passed the Headmaster, greeting parents on their way to the exit.

"Tell the Head, what you told me earlier!"

"Next year I want to be in it!"

The head teacher's face lit up with a genuine smile.

"I will hold you to that," he said warmly, "I hope you will - I will look forward to seeing you up there on the stage!"

One step at a time, I thought, perhaps we had better see how the drama workshop works out first...

A few weeks later, we entrusted him into the hands of an enthusiastic theatre group at a local youth centre for the mix of activities that they had prepared for children with special needs. Ben emerged that afternoon excited and exhilarated. He had had a great time.

At the end of the week, we were invited to arrive early for the show - a mini performance by the children. Each child had prepared an individual 'turn' of their choice with group numbers in dance and song at the beginning and end. The hall was cavernous, drab and bare but they had rigged up a stage area at one end with screens either side for the entrances and exits. The row of twenty or so hard upright chairs was arranged in a semi-circle. The sponsors of the event were there, including a representative of the local social services, alongside parents and siblings kitted with cameras and mobile phones in abundance. There were about four helpers conspicuously shouting cues and encouragement, and around eight children. Each had chosen what they wanted to do, were introduced, performed then exited to loud clapping. The finale was a song and dance routine performed by all the cast and most of the helpers, culminating in each child taking a bow to rapturous applause. Ben performed a karaoke solo over a popular music track, his voice a little thinner than usual but his smile broader than ever. Others sang, danced or told jokes. Every one of their faces told of personal triumph, pride and a distant goal reached. Many moist eyes could be seen amongst that tiny audience in the huge dreary hall. This pilot project was a big success and the stepping stone to more opportunities to follow. This small team of theatre enthusiasts had begun to make a big difference in many children's lives!

The following year I noticed details about the practices for the school production. Ben was still determined that he wanted to take part. I phoned the Drama teacher who said that although he had missed the official audition, she would happily let him join the fifteen-strong chorus. She also warned us that she would be giving him a long list of practices that he must attend.

There followed many weeks of after school practices, learning songs and late pick-ups but Ben knew that to take part, he had to attend them. Whilst his friend dropped out, he kept going, eventually coping with weekend rehearsals and a whole day off timetable for the dress

107

rehearsal. The school had found him a teaching assistant to support him in rehearsals and show nights, helping him with everything from filling the waiting times to changing his costumes and prompting with stage cues.

I think he expected us to be there at every showing but in the event, we attended two nights, Richard and I each taking one of his brothers. The production was lively, fun and entertaining. There were some good individual performances and a few minor snags along the way. Ben played his part, sometimes a fraction behind cue or off the beat, but he was definitely part of the show, contributing to the success of the whole. With the others, he proudly took his bow and revelled in the encore before we collected him, exhausted for the drive home. As we walked towards the exit, I caught the Headmaster's eye. He broke into a warm smile, as he addressed Ben:

"Well done," he said, "You did really well!"

Ben's face glowed with a rare pride. He had done what he set out to do twelve months before. He had reached his first peak!

Later, he took part in a large disability production, a pantomime based on the story of Robin Hood, held at a converted church hall theatre space. He enjoyed the practices and the performance, working with deaf and wheelchair-bound young people and those with Down's syndrome, as well as a supporting group from a local primary school. This role reversal was both effective and poignant as the star roles were given to the children with various forms of disability. Ironically it was the local school children who made mistakes; the special needs children were faultless!

Another year, another production. This time they presented a pantomime combining three well-known children's tales, with the same formula of children with disabilities supported by a minority who had none. On this occasion, however, the performance took place in the largest theatre in town, where we had often seen well-known actors perform. For that one night, they were *the big stars* on a *big stage*. He had realised his dream, he had climbed his mountain!

CHAPTER 21

Cricket

Around the age of ten Ben expressed an interest in playing cricket. With some trepidation, we took him along to a local club. The coaching was excellent and the coaches friendly. He enjoyed the sessions and developed a decent bowling action. During the first year, he played in regular fixtures and made his contribution to the team. The club was running two teams and he played frequently in the 'B' squad. By the next season, it was clear that the 'A' squad featured some talented young players though some of these were only too well aware of this fact. I began to see problems ahead. Whilst the coaches were kind and inclusive, the young players were not.

The highlight of his days here came at the end of an extraordinary fixture, with a team from another area. The match took place at an idyllic ground set in the heart of the English countryside. The clubhouse was quaint and old. There was a beautiful thatched cottage in the far corner of this field, overlooking the pitch beyond the distant boundary. His brother had played here several times before. It held memories of warm summer days and good cricket. The team needed a few runs to win off the last over. Ben was the last batsman to take his place at the crease. Some of the other boys looked at him disparagingly, as if resigned that my son was inevitably going to fail in his task. They were hoping his partner would maintain the strike; they fancied their chances more with the other boy at the crease.

With a few balls to go, Ben took his stand. They held their breath. So did I. I think he missed the first ball. Eyebrows were raised.

"He can make runs, boys, wait and see! "His coach knew he could - but would he deliver under pressure?

Then he struck out for a four. The boys were happy to have the score they needed. They had already forgotten who had made them. I exhaled deeply. My boy! Well done!

Our decision to exit this club was sealed the day I overheard a cruel remark to my son made by one of the top players. Indignant, I reported the incident to the coach.

"Boys will be boys. I don't see there is much I can do."

When we left that day, I knew that we had no future there.

One day I read a notice about a cricket club who welcomed youngsters with special needs. We went along a few times but found little evidence of their claim. After a few weeks, we gave up.

The following year Ben started playing cricket at his secondary school. They held practices three afternoons a week, often for a couple of hours at a time and he loved these sessions. He was chosen for the school team and played in all their fixtures until he left school four years later.

A team from another school in the town contained several members from his former club. One particular afternoon, I sat on the boundary, watching the game and listened to their cruel jibes at my son's expense until I could bear it no longer and I moved out of earshot. We had made the right decision.

Soon afterwards, his PE teacher approached and told us that another local club were looking for members. He invited Ben to attend the club training sessions. He played regularly for this new club, in an atmosphere of tolerance and acceptance. There were three players at this club with disabilities, all playing on a regular basis and making valuable contributions to their teams. Ben was given a special award for his bowling performance one year and enjoyed playing club cricket for the next five seasons. I was proud to sit with the other parents, watching our sons enjoy the games.

Ben could play junior cricket for two additional seasons because of the rules for young cricketers with disabilities. When it was time to move into senior cricket with more overs and harsher rules, he declined the offer. Perhaps he realised that the off-pitch hours would be long and unstructured, though nothing was said. It was as if after his last fixture, he drew a line and turned the page. He was grateful that he had played the game; he had enjoyed himself. Now, he had begun a new chapter. He enjoys watching the cricket highlights on television but his own career had come to its natural end.

CHAPTER 22

The Awards Evening

Moments of pride and pleasure are all the more prized with children who receive few accolades. They are, however, often tinged with irony, humour and distress.

I received a tip-off from two members of the PE department at my son's secondary school:

"Your son has been invited to the School Sports Awards Evening. You *will* make sure he is there, won't you?" A nod and a wink belied the young man's enthusiasm and excitement alongside the evident difficulty he faced in trying to maintain the secrecy of the issue, whilst conveying his message.

"He has been nominated for an award." The words spilled out as he tried to hold himself in check, evidently relieved not to have released all the details, at least. His teachers were clearly proud of what my son had achieved and their part in helping him achieve it.

"Thank you! I will definitely make sure we get him there. When is it?"

"Friday 10th July at 7.30pm in the Sports Hall. Own clothes. A few nibbles. Should be a fun evening."

At the sound of the date, thoughts flooded my mind. My troubled look belied my consternation. Any other Friday would be fine. That weekend, Ben had the rare opportunity to go away with the church youth group. They were leaving around 5.30pm. He could not be at two events simultaneously. How could I break this to him? I did not wish to appear ungrateful but it was evident that at that moment I did not fully enter into this young teacher's enthusiasm. Knowing this would cause Ben much turmoil, I quickly arranged my thoughts to offer a compromise. Richard could offer to take him to the camp destination after the ceremony at school. He would miss the first evening but still be able to enjoy both the Awards Evening and most of the camping weekend. Relief. It was sorted logically, efficiently, decisively in my mind.

When I met Ben, he seemed fine. The school day had gone well. He was at peace with the world. As I was driving home, I began to explain the good news.

"Why have I got to go to an Awards Evening? Why can't they change the date? But I can't go. I'm going away on the youth weekend. They will *have* to change the date."

"But..."

In an instant I am reminded that my logic is entirely different from my son's. To him, this awards evening presented itself as, at best, a major inconvenience. He had completely missed the sense of honour, pride, being chosen. He was going to 'sort it out' with the PE department and tell them they had to change their plans! That was his logical conclusion. At these moments, the sand shifts beneath you and what was fixed with clear natural laws has instantly changed. Someone has switched off the earth's gravitational pull. The irrefutable laws of the universe have been wiped out at a stroke. My safe, predictable afternoon just ended!

A few minutes later, I was being accused of a dozen fictitious crimes of an ever more heinous nature, directed at my son, the world, the universe... He was rocking in the passenger seat next to me, violently kicking the dashboard in front of him and both verbally and physically threatening me. I did not know what to do. I moved onto autopilot. Safety first - stop the car! I pulled over but I did not feel safe: I was in a busy narrow road with a sea wall on one side and a relentless stream of traffic on the other. Next to me the anger and violence continued. I phoned Richard. Straight to answer phone. Alone.

In desperation, I tried to think of anyone else in reach that might be able to help. I was about ten minutes away from the church and the youth leader's office - still too far to drive, but I phoned anyway. To my surprise, he answered with a cheery, friendly voice. He could immediately hear my background noise. I asked him to speak to Ben. Within seconds, they were talking football and teen-life. As a time-traveller in a film, my atmosphere and surroundings were instantly changed. Richard returned my call as soon as the phone was free. He was ten minutes away. I was no longer alone, though I no longer needed his help, at least as long as my surroundings did not change again.

We went to the Awards Evening, as proud parents. Our son picked up awards for several sports in which he had represented the school and a special award for showing 'outstanding commitment and enthusiasm'.

Whilst he enjoyed the walk up the red carpet and the general ambiance, I think the significance and sense of special honour were entirely missed by him. As parents, though, we were very proud. Thank you, teachers and assistants for championing my son's achievements in a world where so often his lack of ability draws the spotlights!

We took him straight from the ceremony to his camping weekend then arrived at around midnight at a B+B. This was a rare chance to enjoy time together, not on this occasion in a Kent farmhouse as we had planned, but a slightly down-market hotel just opposite a railway station, a few miles from his campsite. Still it was clean and quiet and we collapsed into a deep sleep...

CHAPTER 23

The Paper Round and the Puppy

Ben had always wanted to deliver newspapers. He had watched his brother do so and heard of other youngsters busy with their rounds. It sounded possible, a relatively simple task within his grasp, providing I escorted him. We had never allowed him to go out alone because we simply felt he could not deal with the complex demands of traffic, strangers, directions and the unpredictability of life without support. Nevertheless, we were acutely aware of the need to make advances, however small, towards independence. It was a recurrent background theme of the team of professionals we met: independence, the ultimate goal! As parents, too we longed for the freedom that would bring, aware of the milestone it would represent.

Volunteering to take his brother's delivery round one day seemed a good place to start. The task was to deliver booklets. The money earned would be his, but unlike most young people, this was not his motivation. It was to be the satisfaction of achieving something he had wanted to do for some time. The day was cool and dry, the route a little way from our home but in familiar territory. I took the car only to save time and because the booklets were too heavy for a single load. I parked the car, took out the old metal trolley and we began to load it with the thick booklets. He pushed the trolley at my suggestion but complained it was heavy.

"It'll get lighter as we get going," I said cheerfully, unwilling to relieve him of his responsibility at the first hurdle. He looked helplessly at me as we approached the first front door.

"Is there a dog?" he asked, fear enveloping his face.

"I don't know. There will be dogs in some of the houses but not all of them."

I showed him how to insert the books through the letterboxes, without offering fingers as a snack to a potentially rabid or merely enthusiastic canine. He remained unconvinced, the fear overwhelming him as I continued my demonstration for a dozen or so more doors. If the letterbox was too small, we had to knock and hand the booklet personally to an occupant. It was a laborious task which neither of us was enjoying. Eventually I persuaded him to take a turn, myself alongside for moral support, able to take over if needed. He reticently delivered a few, his eyes never leaving me.

Gradually, progress was being made. It was time to replenish the stock with more booklets from my car. We had progressed a few hundred yards from our starting point but were still only around the midpoint of the quiet residential road. Instead of dragging the heavy metal cart back to the car, I decided to move the car to a new parking place. I told him what I was going to do and asked him if he was happy to stay with the trolley and wait a few minutes while I did so. This was the first time he had ever been left alone.

"Just stay there! Don't talk to anyone! I will only be a minute or two. You know where I am. It will save us carrying the heavy trolley back as we can load it up from here."

He was anxious but acquiescent as I walked quickly to the car. The street was deserted. He was standing safely away from the road, propped up against a low wall, guarding the trolley. I felt his eyes follow me, willing my speedy return. As I unlocked my car and climbed in, he was out of sight for a few seconds. The distant sound of an approaching car reached my ears but I did not register any sense of imminent danger. The car passed and I started my engine, following in its wake a few seconds later. The car pulled up a little further along from Ben. I thought nothing of it. The mother stopped her car near her house as the children tumbled out, followed by the family dog; a lively puppy manically flailing in his excitement at finding space and freedom. I was parking my car, unconsciously witnessing these precursory events, feeling safe, totally failing to predict the next few frames in the sequence.

These passed in slow motion in front of me, a few feet away but a lifetime apart. The puppy bounded up to my son, enthusiastically leaping towards him, keen to lick him, to play. Ben, panicked into an involuntary response, ran into the road, chased by the dog interpreting this as a game. I screamed his name, searched the space where an oncoming car could have been and swept him onto the far pavement with an iron embrace. The mother, dragging the dog under control, looked helplessly towards us.

"I'm so sorry. He only wanted to play. He's very friendly. I had no idea…" Her voice trailed, aware of my feelings, of what might have

121

been, of how in a moment a simple everyday domestic scene could have become a tragedy.

We said little but a mother's understanding met in our eyes.

"He's alright," I said. "That's the main thing!"

I sat in the car with him for a moment, trying to sound urgent but calm, explaining that you must *never* run out into the road, that it would be better to be pushed over by a dog than be run over by a car; that most dogs are only trying to be friendly...Even while I was saying these things, I mentally drew a thick black line under the chapter of independence, sure that he was not ready, determined that this chapter would not be opened for a long time. Thanking God, I felt grateful that I still had my son, aware that he needed me and determined that I would be there for him.

He never did ask again to do a paper round.

CHAPTER 24

Threats, Blood and Forty Pairs of Eyes

I cannot remember the trigger. It is as if my video flashback begins at the point of crisis. What I remember is Ben lunging at me menacingly, intent on carrying out his verbal threats of violence and his eldest brother intervening, pushing him aside in my defence. Ben was charging wildly up and down the room. I heard a dull thud as he fell against the edge of the radiator and recall the sight of bright red blood flowing from the wound. I grabbed a towel from the kitchen drawer and held it against his head. It was clear that this required medical attention. The next few minutes passed in a blur of trying to hold the towel in place, preventing Ben from attacking his older brother (who he held responsible) and minimising the blood on the carpet as he chased him up the stairs.

Behind all this frenetic foreground activity, my mind was prioritising the dangers, evaluating the most effective source of help and formulating a strategy to follow. I called Richard who promised to come immediately but I knew he was at least ten minutes away. Ten long minutes. I shouted to my oldest son to lock himself in, assured him, without conviction that I would be alright and tried to convince Ben that he needed to forget everything else and see a doctor 'to make his head better.' I did not want to cause him more anxiety but knew I had to try and break his current pattern of thought; it would be better for him to worry about his cut head. The minutes passed somehow.

He was still wild, shouting, distressed, when Richard arrived. We left immediately, bloodied towels in our hands. He did not calm down on the journey so was very agitated and loud when we arrived at A&E reception. Forty pairs of eyes had already stirred at our dramatic entrance. There was a slow-moving queue of three or four people in front of us at the desk. I apologised for the scene we caused and mentioned to the receptionist that my son was on the autistic spectrum, adding she could check his records if she wished. I asked if she could please process him quickly. She barely looked up, informed me that we would have to wait our turn and stated that if he was likely to behave violently towards the hospital staff they might refuse to treat him.

"So, you would send a young person away with a head wound?" I mumbled, without thinking, half to myself.

"He's much more likely to harm my husband or myself." I said directly to her by way of response.

We waited our turn. She did not hurry - perhaps the accumulated frustration of years spent in her post had drained her ability to feel compassion; she did not seem to have any left that day.

After registering at reception, you were expected to sit in the adjacent waiting area until called. This, as usual was full of patients with a wide range of problems, from those clutching sick bowls to those with bloody rags, from ashen faces to jolly hobblers, sports kits to daywear, babies to the elderly. There was little space here and it was clearly not the best place to take a troubled teenager so Richard took Ben a little way down the adjoining corridor, where he continued to threaten and rant. Things were getting worse. At one point, I approached the desk again:

'If you don't see us soon, you may have more than one casualty to deal with!"

It was not a sarcastic threat, rather a desperate plea for help.

The way we were viewed with apparent disdain from our arrival merely added to our distress. The forty pairs of eyes fixed on this spectacle, a mix of condemnation, disgust and helplessness, accentuated the sense of social exclusion. Surrounded by a crowd, totally alone!

Eventually, we were called. A quick glance confirmed the need for gluing the deep cut. I winced as I wondered how Ben would cope with the sting of cleansing the wound, followed by the act of pushing the two sides together to apply the cold, liquid glue. But a switch had shifted in his mindset as we had entered the treatment room. Ben, suddenly calm, talked sensibly to the doctor then heroically displayed stoicism and courage in the face of the pain before calmly exiting to the surprise of the incredulous onlookers.

Richard and I exhausted, his eldest brother shocked to have witnessed things he had not imagined possible; Ben quiet and proud of his bravery, we went home to bed. Another kind of ordinary!

CHAPTER 25

The Social Worker

I could never be a social worker. So much need, so little resources, so many impossible decisions. I would begin wanting to change the world and end in despair.

At some point in the course of events, Ben was assigned a social worker. He was an amiable gent, easy to talk to, and genuinely interested in people. His specialism was young people with autism and he understood the way they think. He worked hard on our behalf to help us obtain the necessary support in education and arranged for us to have the services of a carer for two hours a week. He attended a number of meetings, with school, local authority representatives, educational psychologists and the medical profession. He also helped us to obtain a bus pass for my son and an escort. He visited us at approximately six monthly intervals and my son enjoyed seeing him. They established a mutual interest in football and table tennis in their first encounter and always bantered around these topics before discussing other things. He usually spent a brief time with me discussing how things were going before Ben joined us.

From time to time our case was reassessed and we had to justify afresh our need. On one occasion, we were in danger of losing our carer allocation. An eloquent letter from one of my carers, in support of our case resulted in no change being implemented. The situation was a complex game of cat and mouse with the social services eyeing their ever-decreasing budget and our family keen to claw on to the little help we had. Mutual respect existed between us, alongside an awareness of our different perspectives.

The moment that I really understood the function of the social worker and the limited options available to him came the morning after Ben had struck his brother, an expression of his frustration about something unrelated to his sibling. I phoned our social worker. I felt desperate. I could not live with the fact that unprovoked my son could inflict potentially serious and lasting damage on one of my other children. I was appalled by the previous day's event and wanted solutions. I do not know what I expected the social worker to do but I think I was hoping for practical as well as moral support.

"Something has to happen," I railed," We cannot go on like this! Does it have to take a serious incident for you to do something?"

"What do you want me to do?"

The effect of his question was chilling as I realised with a mixture of horror and profound isolation that the only thing he could offer me was to take my child into care. I knew this would only make things much worse; so did the social worker.

"*I am not asking you to take him in to care,*" I replied, suddenly in full control.

"We will manage, somehow."

In that moment, I realised that there was nothing more out there. That no one had answers to our situation. That we had to go it alone because there was no other way. There was no quick fix; there would never be a cure. People might offer sticking plasters or bandages but the wound would never fully heal!

Even sticking plasters are gratefully received and we are profoundly grateful to the friends, school, youth leaders, church members and family who have offered their help in different ways. Their kindness makes the day to day easier and lessens the immensity of the chasm. Thank you also to the social services and their limited help. I would not have your job.

CHAPTER 26

The Honeymoon That Lasted Five Minutes Too Long

One of my father's last gifts to me before his death nine months later was a second honeymoon.

"You need a real break away, something special, we will look after Ben for a few days to give you time to have a full week's holiday somewhere away from it all."

My parents knew that Ben was booked to go to camp with the church youth group for five days that summer which was our chance to have a holiday. They also knew that we could not go far because of the limited time and dates available. If they looked after Ben for a few days after the camping trip, we could take a full week's break. We thought about it, weighed up the pros and cons then started to look at available holiday options. We had rarely taken holidays abroad during our thirty-year marriage primarily because of the cost but at this time we had recently inherited some money and this offer to look after our son gave us the opportunity to go abroad.

We chose a holiday on Italy's Lake Garda, in a family-run hotel with superb food, an outdoor pool with a backdrop of snow-capped mountains, close to the edge of the lake on the road leading into the sleepy town of Torbole, a few minutes' walk away. The holiday was perfect: the weather glorious, the scenery chocolate-box beautiful, the food exquisite but more importantly we gradually began to relax. Every morning we woke to the prospect of choice - we could do what we liked, when we chose or we could choose to do nothing. We had no restrictions, no obligations and no constraints. In fact, apart from a special day trip to Venice when we followed the tourist trail, we just relaxed, walking, taking local boat trips to other settlements, swimming daily in the pool or lake, dressing up for dinner, playing table tennis in the sunshine of the hotel's garden. It was blissful, altogether more spectacular than our original honeymoon which though pleasant, had been a budget affair in a humble Yorkshire guest house.

We took regular texts and some calls from Ben and my parents but mostly we stopped feeling solely responsible, knowing we were far away and trusted those in charge. He was having a good time and in the care of able individuals who knew and loved him. For a short time, we began to let go.

We flew back to Gatwick, collected our car and drove home, tired from the travelling but exhilarated by the break. The arrangement was that we would drive to meet my parents at a hotel approximately half way between their home and ours on the M4 corridor at 4pm the following day, enjoy an early meal with my parents, then depart in different directions.

I suppose it was precisely because we had relaxed and enjoyed such a good time, that Richard was caught off-guard the following day. He woke refreshed and began to pick the apples from our heavily-laden fruit tree. He became absorbed in the task and wanted to finish it. I did remind him but I think he honestly thought we would have a quick, relatively traffic-free journey around the M25. So we left late. Then we met a lot of traffic. We made several phone calls to Ben and my parents but we could only apologise, say we were on our way, say we were trying our best.

Our best was not good enough that day. We had failed him and my parents and we were all to pay a heavy price. As we drove up the long drive to the hotel, I saw my mother and Ben in the distance, looking out towards the drive, anticipating our arrival. As the long driveway swept around, I momentarily lost sight of them both. In that brief moment, everything changed.

As planned, Ben had spent five days camping with the church youth group at a large event with many other similar groups. He had enjoyed the fresh air, the cooked breakfasts, freedom within the boundary of the closed site, the gatherings, the casual games of football, the plentiful supply of cakes, chocolate and friendly acceptance. As arranged, my parents had met him with the group leader at 9pm, taken his bag and left with him to a local Travelodge where they had booked a family room. Ben loves hotels and chatted excitedly about his adventures until he fell deeply asleep. They returned home the next morning to my parents' home in Wales, stopping on the way for lunch at a restaurant. Ben loves eating in restaurants. He was well-behaved, grateful and happy.

The following morning, after throwing the newly washed clothes into his bag, he left with them in the back of the car, expectant and cheerful. They stopped once on their journey, to eat the picnic feast that my mother had prepared, before arriving at the four-star hotel, our rendezvous, at around 2 o'clock. My parents had booked a room for the night, so were shown to a luxurious double, decorated in chintz, with antique furniture, a cottage-feel and a stunning view of the extensive grounds. This was an English country house, tastefully transformed into a luxury hotel, in a peaceful rural setting on a pleasant August day.

As my father was tired, my mother took my son for a walk in the grounds, playing croquet on the lawn, having waited their turn patiently, as other guests completed their game. They returned to the room in good spirits to enjoy a drink and watch some television, aware because of our calls and texted updates that we were running late. Ben wanted to watch the programme of his choice but my parents said they wanted to watch a news bulletin first. Although he did not react visibly at this time, the first rumblings deep within were beginning to stir, the unseen forewarning of the explosive eruption to follow…

They received my text informing them that we were approaching the hotel drive. My mother offered to come down to the driveway to meet us and direct us to the annexe building.

"I want to come too."

"That's fine, let's go down to meet mummy and daddy together."

A few minutes later, they emerged at the entrance to the courtyard, at the far extremity of the long drive, past the main house and the hotel's reception.

Whether Ben expected us to be waiting for them in the courtyard, or the toll of our delay was too great; or the disappointment of being made to wait for his television programme or a thousand little insecurities stored from the past week caused the explosion to erupt that minute, we can only guess, but in between my first and second glimpses of him from the car window, something happened: he hit my mother hard across her shoulder.

Instantly, he knew he had done something terrible. Instantly, he felt remorse but expressed it in ever-increasing agitation. My mother was stunned, sad, fearful, gracious, understanding and forgiving. Richard spent the next few hours and most of the next week talking to Ben, calming him, trying to help him regain equilibrium. We shared a corporate feeling of guilt, failure, regret but we all knew things could never be the same again: a chasm into the unthinkable had been breached. I could never again leave him alone with his grandparents. My parents' concern for our safety and our future increased greatly.

Before my father died, I promised him that I possess the courage to make the most difficult choice, if ever I have to. I cannot imagine entrusting my son to the care of others for his safety and our own but I know sometimes, for some families it is the only choice... I pray I never have to make that decision. I hope he was reassured. I meant what I said.

Thank you Mum and Dad for my honeymoon!

I never left Ben alone with them again.

CHAPTER 27

I Hope You Crash the Car!

As we got into the car, I knew Ben was edgy. It was always a gamble taking him the twenty-minute drive to the centre for an activity he loved. If I did not take him, the situation would explode at home. Now, I took the risk it could explode elsewhere. I carried on, not because I was brave but because I could not think clearly; not because I felt optimistic but because a passive fatalism had taken over.

We bundled in to the car and I manoeuvred the vehicle in silence for a while. Then I tried to enter into chit-chat as if everything was normal. We were approaching the turning to leave the built-up area and take a deserted country lane when the escalation began. I do not think it was planned to coincide with the physical isolation; Ben did not process ideas that systematically. It merely intensified my sense of hopelessness and distance from everyone else's world.

"You are always grumpy, aren't you?"

"No. I'm not grumpy."

"Yes, you are and you are always horrible to me."

"I don't think that is fair because I am not grumpy and I do a lot of things for you. I am taking you now to your riding lesson because I know you like it."

The irony of the moment was not lost on my racing brain - although I had started out perfectly calmly, after his accusations, I began to feel agitated. 'Please be quiet', I thought, 'I need mind space.' I also needed to concentrate on steering around the twisting country lane. The last thing I needed now was to crash the car.

"I am not going to talk for a while. I must concentrate on driving. I want us to be safe."

I often said this to him whilst travelling in the car. I do not enjoy driving and I have to focus fully on the process. He was used to it. Sometimes it made him stop talking for a while. Other times I have stopped the car for reasons of safety; this always enflamed him. It did however, avoid traffic accidents.

"I hope you crash the car!"

Has your child ever said that to you? What would you do? This comment pierced all my default mechanisms. It did not make me angry, so much as very sad - that profound emotion that twists and wounds on the inside. 'This should not happen,' I thought. 'I love you but sometimes you make that so very hard.'

As we arrived at our destination, I was aware that one of two outcomes would be inevitable. I hoped, without faith, that the change of surroundings and the prospect in hand would deflect Ben's attention from our current crisis. The alternative would be beyond embarrassment and change forever the people's perception of my son in this place. Dispassionately, mechanically, I helped Ben put on his riding helmet and presented him to the instructor. I chose not to watch the class but to retreat to my car. This gave me precious mind space and some physical distance between us.

At the end of the class, he returned, a different persona. I, still smarting from my inner wound, exchanged pleasantries and started the car. About a quarter of a mile further on, he turned to me.

"Sorry, mum."

For Ben, the event was over. Those magic words were the end of the issue. Like an advert for a cleaning product, the mark was wiped away, the surface glinting in the light, as new. But for me, the internal wound remained. I responded gradually but without feeling. If I did not, the events of the outward journey would surely be repeated. How do you tell an autistic child that life is not always like the advert?

CHAPTER 28

Medication

I had read, with that universal distant interest and sympathy common to all parents, about drugs like *Ritalin* and the dilemma of parents asked to choose between the polar stereotypes of uncontrollable children without medication and zombie-like children on ever-increasing amounts of strong drugs. I never imagined that one day I might be contemplating similar issues.

Things had been deteriorating. The stress of changing schools and the onset of puberty had brought the combination of anxiety, aggression and greater physical strength with the newly acquired vocabulary of a secondary school playground. This combined to form potent outbursts of verbal threats and physical aggression. A table tennis bat was thrown across the room at me, leaving a permanent, deep indentation on my living room wall. My other son had been struck on the head in an angry outburst. All sharp or heavy objects were removed for safe keeping, including with great sadness, the removal of all Ben's sports trophies from display.

Richard and I found ourselves across a room from a child psychiatrist we had never met before discussing the two options available: either to pursue behavioural therapy, which he suggested probably would not work because of my son's low cognitive scores, or to commence treatment with a similar drug to *Ritalin*. We were read an interminable list of potential side-effects and problems and invited to make a decision. We asked for time as this was such a momentous choice. We took the prescription, were given a dummy sample to see the size of the tablet and left, stunned. We took a while to reach our conclusion, having searched the internet on medical, pharmaceutical and parental websites for information and opinions until we realised we were reading the same details over and over again but no-one would actually make a decision for us[1]. Although our situation was far from acceptable, we concluded it was not yet at the point where we felt desperate enough to commit our child to such a drastic measure. The prescription remained, unused on our kitchen notice board.

In fact, we did nothing until our next appointment when we were greeted by a different face, a new consultant and a different opinion. He explained that the original prescription was not in his opinion the most appropriate, instead he suggested a different drug and a series of meetings with a psychologist to try out behavioural therapy. This encounter was at once unnerving and reassuring. Initially, we felt unnerved that the decision we had agonised over had been irrelevant. This instant change of opinion in such a short time, presented by an equally qualified medical consultant momentarily destroyed our faith in the whole system. It also made me think how betrayed we would have

---

1   My research revealed that many of these drugs are not licensed for use on children, an alarming fact apparently common to many medicines prescribed for children on account of the difficulty of setting up reliable trials.

felt if we had reached a different conclusion. However, it was reassuring to have someone who was willing to respect our reticence and try out therapy. He also told us about other medication which we might consider if this failed.

The therapy sessions were interesting and helpful and Ben liked and trusted the psychologist. However, as had been feared, lasting change was limited. By the time we went for our next meeting with the psychiatrist, we knew difficult questions would be posed. As before, the psychiatrist asked our views on starting medication. He explained the risks, both short and long term, promised close monitoring and frequent reviews if we decided to try the treatment. He also told us that this was a temporary measure and he would not plan for Ben to take this drug indefinitely. We had already experienced two major incidents at home. Richard suggested waiting for one more major episode to occur before committing ourselves. The psychiatrist asked him two telling questions:

"What would that change?"

"Is it worth the risk?"

In the silence that followed we knew we had no plausible answers. Several thoughts simultaneously flooded my mind. This cannot go on. How could we forgive ourselves if he damaged someone else's life? What would happen to him if he badly injured us? We knew that we must never allow that to happen, that the safety of others is the most important thing. Our routine at home would soon be disrupted by the return of my two other sons from college, a stressful change for Ben providing a potential flashpoint. I glanced at Richard. There was not much to be said; we both knew what we had to do. Reluctantly we took the consultant's advice, leaving with our first prescription. It was a few days before Christmas.

I slowly opened the box containing the clear fluid in a medicine bottle. I started carefully reading the long leaflet of medical warnings and contraindications then snapped my gaze away. This watery fluid could do any number of things to an individual and nobody would say what or take any responsibility if anything went wrong. In the end, they would all say it was our decision and any consequences would be both our fault and our responsibility.

It was Christmas Eve, the night of the year when children were the most important members of any household. It was a time when innocence was triumphed and sacrifices were made, as adults everywhere acceded to their children the place of primary importance. At least in most homes. At least for one night. So, I felt doubly condemned for putting myself and other adults first on this special night. I felt about to deceive and potentially poison my dear son. I felt that this would be an act of pre-meditated betrayal with far-reaching and perhaps devastating consequences.

But I had made my decision and I knew I must not waiver. I slowly released the unseen liquid into the glass and offered my son his usual milk and a small bowl of cornflakes. He drank it innocently, trusting as he would. I watched and waited. He showed no sign of detecting any difference. He did what he usually did. The deed is done, I thought.

The next day, Christmas Day, he was subdued and by the evening complaining of feeling queasy. We were unsure whether he was succumbing to the prevalent stomach virus or suffering side-effects of the drug. We stopped the drug. After the Bank holidays, we phoned the consultant who returned our call promptly. He suggested we start again at a much lower dose, gradually increasing to the original level. We followed his instructions but did not raise the dose that far. The results were dramatic and remarkable. He was calmer, had greater concentration and no further visible side effects.

As time progressed and Ben grew in size, the dose was adjusted up but never to the original level. Incidents did occur but less frequently and mostly with less aggression than before. He continued to have close monitoring, including regular blood tests as well as consultations.

Then at one regular appointment, the consultant suggested lowering the dose to work towards stopping this medication altogether. We were shocked, disarmed and almost fearful of returning to the previous position, the polar opposite of where we had begun. This consultant, however, had been as good as his word, keeping his promise to be available to us when needed, to monitor our child closely and to use powerful drugs for a limited time, only when other avenues had been exhausted. We felt listened to and cared for with diligence and professionalism, at last!

We suggested waiting until the next appointment. Then gradually we began the process of reducing the dose. To date we have arrived at the minimum therapeutic dose. Further reduction seemed to have a clear negative effect so we had to backtrack, but we have begun the process. One day we hope he will be able to live without medication.

CHAPTER 29

The Forgotten Grade Sheet

It was always going to be a rush. Ben arrived home around 3.45pm and the parents' evening began at 4.30 sharp. The journey would take about 30 minutes. This was the first full week back after the summer holidays and his blazer was now at least two sizes too small. The annual school photograph was to take place the following day at midday and he needed a new blazer. Unfortunately, I had not realised this before the start of term and the school uniform shop was at the other end of town, en route to his school. We wanted to arrive at the parents' evening on time. I wanted to arrive safely and not drive too fast. The plan to go to the parents' evening via a brief stop at the uniform shop was possible but always risky. You do not rush an autistic teenager!

We might have been successful in our risky venture, had I not made a carefree comment concerning the fact that I had left his report sheet at home.

"That was silly," I said, almost to myself, "I meant to pick up your report sheet. Never mind, I am sure the teachers will have their own copies."

The damage was done. My son perseverated interminably about my misdemeanour.

"You should have remembered!"

"You've ruined my day now."

"Go back and get it!"

"All the other people will have their sheets."

"We'll *have* to go back and get it!"

"You always let me down!"

With great remorse at allowing myself to let the comment slip and a desperate effort to remain unruffled and prevent a major escalation of events, I tried to appeal for calm.

"It won't matter. The teachers will have their own copies. Perhaps we will be able to get a spare from them. I'm sure we won't be the only people who forget."

"We can't go back now, that would make us late. It is better to be on time, even without the grade sheet, than be late or miss the parents' evening altogether."

I suppose it is natural to appeal to reasoned, logical thought at these moments. It is futile.

Ben was like a lion guarding his kill. He had only one instinctive urge. My weapon was useless, if not inflammatory.

Again, I tried to retain an appearance of calm.

"Would you like me to take you home instead?"

"Would you like me to phone Dad to pick you up?"

Whilst Ben hates this suggestion because it brings with it a sense of shame, I did so if a situation was tipping into a place where I was fearful for my safety or his. Richard has an ability to calm him that I do not possess. He is also physically larger. What I was acutely aware of was that he was probably at that moment driving from work to meet us at the school, thus unlikely to answer his phone.

By this time, I had parked the car outside the uniform shop and I made the decision to go in, hoping that a physical change of environment might provide a distraction. It did not. He continued haranguing me in the shop in front of other customers and the shop staff. He raised his hand as if to hit me but I moved out of reach. He followed me menacingly around in the shop as we tried to find the correctly sized blazer. No-one in the shop said anything but I felt the burning heat of disapprobation. In the event, I had to order a blazer for collection the following morning as I could not wait the fifteen minutes or so required to attach the necessary school badge.

We left the shop. As we climbed into the car, he still very angry, myself very apprehensive, he issuing forth a torrent of threats and accusations, myself silently despairing, I told him I could only drive on if there was silence, as I needed to concentrate to drive.

I do not remember much about the ten-minute journey from the shop to the school but we went to the parents' evening. On arriving, we were presented with some individual information sheets, including his grades. Richard joined us shortly after our arrival. We heard glowing reports of his hard work and enthusiasm at school and we all felt justifiably proud of his achievements. His anger abated, though it was to resurface a few days later.

I collected the blazer the next morning, offering a brief apology and explanation of my son's condition to the assistant I remembered from the day before.

"You know best what to do." She said without emotion, which merely reminded me that I did not know at all.

I drove the fifty-minute round trip to give it to him at school in time for the photograph. When this arrived a few weeks later, it was unremarkable, though the blazer did look smart.

Neither he, nor I had fully calmed from this event which turned out to be the precursor of something more, when a few days later we went to the cinema.

CHAPTER 30

The Assault at The Cinema

The consultant had encouraged us to try reducing the medication. We wanted to do so very gradually so instead of taking one tablet morning and evening, we began to give a half tablet at night whilst continuing to give a full dose at breakfast. It seemed a reasonable plan. The effects were clearly evident almost from the start. Ben was edgy, irritable and irascible. We felt we had to give it a while at the lower dose; it seemed precipitous to act after a few days, despite the growing unease we felt. After ten days on this reduced amount, we decided to return to the original dose and contacted the consultant. He agreed with our decision. However, this drug takes a few days to regulate within the system, as the effect is cumulative.

The parents' evening when I had forgotten the grades sheet had taken place a few days before. Although Ben was calmer, he was still agitated and we all knew that a flare-up was possible.

That Tuesday was one of those occasional days off for his school, so he had a whole day at home. Originally, we were going to go swimming. The story might have been different if we had stuck to our original plan. Instead, I offered to take him to the cinema instead, thinking this might be more of a treat. The film he chose was only shown at four in the afternoon. This meant that we had a considerable amount of chill-time before the treat arrived. The morning came and went with us both busy doing our own things.

We had lunch together and I began to get organised. As often happens when you think you have much time, something comes up, you misjudge the interval and before you know it, time is short. We had to drop a file off to my husband's car on the way which involved a minor detour and traffic was heavy. We had time to arrive for the start of the film but little to spare. My son knew I was concerned about being late and a little cross with myself. He always feeds on my agitation, thus increasing his own.

Before we left, I had gathered the 3D glasses, cinema card and drink near the front door ready to take. At the last minute, we had thrown them into a tote bag and put them in the car. As I was approaching the car park, I asked him to take out the glasses to save time later. He could not find them.

"You've left them at home."

"It's your fault!"

"You always let me down."

"We can't go now."

"It's OK, I'll buy some new ones. It won't cost much. It's fine!"

"But what about all those pairs at home, what are we going to do about them? We should go and get them."

"If we do, we will miss the film. It's not a big deal; we will get some new ones!"

His agitation was increasing; the spring was coiled.

I parked the car and walked him briskly the few hundred yards to the cinema, hopeful that if I could once get him inside, he might be distracted into a changed mood. The foyer was deserted but for several assistants, manning various tills. I purchased the tickets, paid the extra pound for the new glasses and turned to cross the foyer to the stairs leading to our cinema showing.

As I turned away from the till, he rushed at me. It was a culmination of his increasing frustration. He pushed me hard sideways. I sprawled on the floor, my shoes landing individually a short distance from me. The cinema assistants who had witnessed the event asked me if I was alright and the one who had just served me immediately came over. I rushed to my feet, shocked but eager to assure myself and these strangers that I was OK and to retrieve some dignity. Having established that I was not badly hurt, the assistant turned to us and said calmly:

"I will refund your money."

He then went about doing so, explaining to his manager what had occurred, clicking buttons, inputting figures, whilst I gazed intently, incredulously at Ben who had begun to utter an apology.

"I'm sorry, I'm sorry."

"I can't take you to see the film now."

153

For the briefest moment of time, concepts flashed through my brain. Shock. Despair. A feeling that a line had just been crossed followed by the correction that this line had been crossed a long time before.

After the initial seconds, there is no time to think about yourself. My focus became strategies to get through the next few minutes, half hour, evening. How do I get him safely out of here, back to my car, drive home? I knew the pattern. He was still edgy. He might have said sorry but he probably still believed it was my fault, blaming me for his disgrace. A difficult evening lay ahead. I was grateful that the young man had arranged the refund - not on account of the money but because his action had made it clear to Ben that staying to see the film was not an option. This obviated the perception that *I* had withheld his treat. We walked slowly back to the car park where I phoned Richard. He collected him and I drove home alone.

"I have been assaulted today." I composed in my imaginary diary entry. Then turned the page and continued with real life.

A multi-coloured bruise appeared under my left knee in the following days. I replaced my scuffed shoes. My son frequently asked when the film would be released on DVD as he was keen to see it. I later found the original glasses in the tote bag where they had been with us all through these events.

A few months on, I took Ben to see a film at the same cinema. As I entered, the memory of that day vividly returned to me. I pushed it aside and continued. He seemed to have no recollection. We purchased our tickets and watched the film. Another day!

The Chasm

Nothing prepares you for being hit by your child.
It is not the physical pain;
It is the emotional wound that never heals;
The unspeakable shame of an act
That should never happen.
I have the strength to walk away,
Show dignity, defiance
But my attacker is a vulnerable, frightened child
Struggling with the body and emotions
Of an angry adolescent,
Dependent on my love and affection.
I have no choice; there is no other path,
Only a new day tomorrow.

You cannot understand how I feel,
The double-sided anguish of despair
And knowing that carrying on
Is the only hope.
In that moment, I live
On the other side of the world,
Separated by language, culture and experience,
In a place inhabited without consent
By a chosen few.

CHAPTER 31

London 2012

A great cheer rose from our family when the 2012 Olympic Games were awarded to London on July 6th 2005. It was one of those occasions in your life when you remember where you were, who you were with and what you were doing. As a family, we love sport and both watch and participate in many different sports at various levels. On that occasion, we were in the Clubhouse at a junior county cricket match, surrounded by like-minded individuals. The roar was deafening, followed by hugs and smiles. No sign here of complaints about the cost - we were united in celebration of this once-in-a-lifetime event.

Six years later and still a year before the XXX Olympiad, we made our on-line applications for various tickets. This was my middle son's idea and we applied for many different events at various prices. Had we received all we had requested, the family finances would have been in serious disarray, but I was assured this was not going to happen! In fact, every member of our family attended at least one event, though only Ben and I went to the Olympic Park.

It was a late decision to apply for Paralympics tickets a few weeks before the event that afforded us this privilege. We had evening tickets for the main stadium but decided to go for the whole day and see as much as we could of the Olympic Park. I secretly hoped we might be able to see other events that were taking place there but every event was a sell-out. The nation had embraced the Paralympics with unprecedented enthusiasm, spurred on by the daily television coverage and the excitement of the recent Olympic events. For many, including ourselves the Paralympics gave an opportunity denied by the scarcity of tickets for the Olympics to walk around the Olympic Park itself, to feel part of history!

The last-minute preparations for the day out took longer than expected. I was slightly impatient and Ben does not hurry. I wanted to leave as early as possible to enjoy as much time at the Olympic Park as we could. As we got into the car to go to the train station, it began. The barrage of verbal assault directed at me. I remember thinking that really he did not deserve to go for an amazing day out after this. I knew that my day would only get worse if I refused. I also desperately wanted to go myself. I decided to blank everything out and hope that things would improve. I told myself that trying to hurry him up had probably aggravated him, aware that the whole day contained several unknown elements that made him more liable to outbursts. I felt sorry for myself for an instant, allowing myself an indulgent 'Why me/ I shouldn't have to put up with this' moment, then told him I had to be quiet to drive and he would have to be calm to go to the Paralympics.

I remember little about the remainder of the journey, except that I think it involved him eating some of the more indulgent part of his lunch and me praying that the day would not continue as it had begun.

When we finally reached the Olympic Park, it was swirling with people, heading in all directions, carefully and kindly marshalled by a vast workforce of smiling volunteers. Having discovered that we did not have access to most individual events and buildings on the site, we set about enjoying a walk around the landscaped park itself, identifying key buildings that we had seen on television. I noted food outlets that we hoped to return to later, visited the official shop where we bought some badges as souvenirs, before settling on a grassy bank near the big screen to eat our packed lunch and watch Ellie Simmonds gain a medal in the swimming. The weather was beautiful; not too hot or too cold. Ben was calm enough to enjoy the day, so I could also.

I carried a sense of history, being there, feeling part of something I would be proud to tell my future grandchildren. At one point I stopped to take a photograph of an overview of the Park. You had to wait for your moment as inevitably people kept walking in front of you. I had already waited a few minutes. Ben was getting agitated. He wanted to hurry back to Macdonald's, a highlight of his trip. Just a minute or so longer and I could have taken the perfect picture, the Olympic landmarks with a red London bus in the distance, but I knew the risk of delay would be too great. I snapped my souvenir picture without the red bus and hurried on to rescue the day.

As Ben had been looking forward to his Macdonald's meal, I too had promised myself a baked potato which particularly appealed to me from one of the other food outlets. The idea was that we would buy his meal first then mine before we found a spot to sit down and enjoy eating our food together. When we arrived at Macdonald's, our faces dropped. The queues were some 30 deep at each till. The wait seemed endless. In the end, I kissed goodbye to my mouth-watering baked potato and grabbed the only thing I would eat from the Macdonald's menu, a 'healthy' wrap! We ate our food quickly in the crowded restaurant and took our place in the stadium just in time for the evening programme of events. Below us we could see the cauldron burning with the Olympic flame as from our high vantage point near the top of the stadium you could see running, throwing and jumping events taking place below. As you looked around, the stadium was full. The atmosphere was indescribable, the sense of universal respect for sport and for each competitor omnipresent. If you closed your eyes for a moment you could transport yourself back a few short weeks to Super Saturday, when Team GB won three gold medals and seemed to have conquered the world! I knew it was a privilege to be there. I was grateful that my prayers had been answered.

For Ben, I think the sense of history was absent. His high points were the Macdonald's treat and the novelty of standing up every time a National Anthem was played at the many medal ceremonies that took place during the evening, but he enjoyed it in his own way and we both arrived home that night tired but happy, with much to tell of our special day. I was so glad we had made it.

CHAPTER 32

Dreams and Reality - our Experience of Disability Sport

After witnessing the triumph and recognition afforded to the 2012 Paralympics, it would be easy to assume that opportunities for gifted individuals with disabilities are plentiful and easy to find. Nothing could be further from the truth in my experience. In the autumn of 2012, in the afterglow of that amazing orgy of sport, opportunity and national pride, Ben was proud to receive a letter inviting him to attend a taster event at an athletics track twenty miles from our home. He had been nominated by his school as a potential paralympic hopeful. It was a talent-spotting event. The pride we felt was immense. Imagine how deflated we felt to receive news shortly before this event that it had been cancelled. We were told that it would probably be rescheduled, that we would be informed. We had no further communication. After a few months had elapsed I phoned the number on the headed letter. I was told that the event was not going to be rescheduled. It had been axed. If I was interested, there might be a similar event later in the year some fifty miles away. I think I requested details but our paralympic dream never reached the starting blocks.

We did regularly attend an annual sports event run by the local Rotary Club but linked for a while to the paralympic label. Ben attended with his disability football club and enjoyed taster sessions in many sports including archery, pétanque, javelin, shot-put and fencing as well as fiercely fought competitions in football and table tennis. The final medal ceremony was long as medals were awarded for each event in several different categories. Ben regularly won the table tennis tournament easily against players of varied talent but great enthusiasm. However, there was no talent-spotting here, merely an opportunity for participation. It always left me wondering how individuals moved from this to serious competitive disability sport.

Perhaps one of the biggest hindrances is that of access to training and events. Since disabled people are in the minority, the local talent pool in any given sport and the number of sports clubs for them is less than for individuals without disabilities. This means that they will need to travel farther to access facilities but individuals with disabilities are less independent so travelling greater distances is harder for them. Parents often juggle dealing with their other children and their social activities so few have the willingness or opportunity to even start along the trail. To a certain extent, I feel it is a postcode lottery; individuals who live closer to better facilities have greatly increased choices and chances. Sometimes availability depends on matching criteria - I was informed that our local athletics club catered for sportsmen and women with physical issues but not other disabilities. The alternative remains to join ordinary clubs but in practice this often leads to isolation, taunting and being overlooked perhaps because complex instructions were not understood, unusual behaviour was displayed or for a lack of social skills.

I had been informed that individuals on the autistic spectrum are eligible for the Special Olympics. I knew nothing about these events or of any entry procedures for inclusion into their orbit until Ben's football club recently started up a Special Olympics squad which he has joined. For other sports, I remain unaware. We may have advanced a long way as the 2012 Paralympic Games demonstrated but opportunities are by no means equal or procedures for consideration widely known amongst families of disabled individuals. There is much yet to be done!

....

Our experience in the world of disability football however, has been a different story. When Ben first expressed a desire to join a football club and 'play proper fixtures like his older brother', my heart sank. I did not believe that his experiences at an average club would be positive. I was only too well aware of how intolerant parents and youth players could be. Yet when we investigated the possibility of a disability football club, the alternatives were few. It came down to a club some twenty minutes' drive out of town, another in a different town completely or an embryonic side composed of individuals with all forms of disabilities from wheelchair-bound to learning difficulties and autism. This is where we began since it was the closest to home. However, it took only a few sessions to realise that this was not going to work for Ben. He was repeatedly being asked to tone down the powerful kick he had developed so as not to put a wheelchair user at risk. To me it seemed unfair to both individuals to continue. We tried the second option.

When we first took Ben to this disability football club, we were concerned about the distance we would need to travel. Once we had watched him enjoy himself so much, in an atmosphere of encouragement and acceptance, we never turned back.

From the moment we arrived, we felt a sense of acceptance, a sense of belonging. Here people never asked questions which had no answers or stared if any child had a bad day. Here was a tacit complicity, a sense of community, an absence of judgement, a place of safety. We have belonged to this community for many years now. Ben enjoys the training, the tournaments, the social events, the sense of belonging to a group, the familiarity of the environment. With this community, we have been on a camping holiday at an outdoor activity centre; watched the local town football matches; been to Wembley stadium; watched the England U19 team; enjoyed fund-raising meals; sold cakes, burgers and bacon butties, mourned two deaths and seen coaches and families come and go. However, the core of this group has remained very loyal and stable. The main coach, adored by the young players has an understanding of these individuals and their issues and an infectious love of football and its enabling freedom. Its value is far greater than an hour or two of physical exercise per week. This is not just a football club, this is a community. Its effect on these lives is not limited to football skills; it brings confidence, self-worth and freedom to vulnerable young adults, and fun and friendship to parents and families.

Next summer we are looking forward to going to the UK Special Olympics in Sheffield, where Ben and his team are competing. The team, coach and helper are going to stay on a university campus whilst many of us parents have booked self-catering or bed and breakfast accommodation nearby. There will be an opening ceremony and medals in each event. The most successful competitors will be chosen to represent Team GB in the next International Special Olympics. For Ben, the significance of the Olympic label is lost. For him, it is a big adventure, a sort of football holiday with his club, even at times a mild inconvenience. When we are there, I know he will love it but the build-up seems long and complicated - not least the need to fundraise to meet the several hundred pounds' fee for each player to take part and the copious amount of forms that have to be filled in. For us as parents, it is another milestone which we will celebrate with pride.

CHAPTER 33

The Work Experience Placement

Ben's work experience had been planned long before the event. Two friends had started up a café business some years before and they had promised us that he could do his work experience placement there. They had a wealth of experience with young people of all abilities and regularly received students on work experience. We visited the café several times before he started his two-week placement. He had spent a few hours before helping at the church café but this was a more formal atmosphere. The menu was varied with a wide range of fare from breakfasts, homemade cakes and snacks to cooked lunches. We realised from the outset that Ben would not be able to handle the till or take complex orders at the tables. What he was able to do was serve, wash up, clear tables and speak to customers.

When I took him for a trial run, a few weeks before, the café owners asked me to stay to give him confidence and to advise them what tasks he could and could not undertake. He had to put on his apron and was informed where everything was kept. Fire regulations and basic safety procedures were explained. Then the work began. I tried to remain inconspicuous, sitting in a quiet corner. I took a book and passed my time reading and chatting with both the staff and customers. I even offered to do some washing up to pass the time.

The first task he was given was to take a hot drink order to a customer.

"You are ok carrying hot drinks, aren't you?" inquired the owner nonchalantly as she placed the steaming cup on the delivery tray. It was a hurried question, with little opportunity for response. I wondered what was going to happen next as at the church café, he had recently said no to an identical question. There, he had to date only carried cold drinks and sandwiches. Ben took a deep breath then carried the tray tentatively to the table. From then on, he carried trays of hot and cold drinks and food. I could see he was going to benefit from this experience.

In my planning, I had marked down the work experience fortnight as a welcome relief from the usual early start for school and a time when Ben would be busy for most of the day. In the event, the café owners felt that he would struggle with working during the peak times and suggested he work mornings only from ten to twelve. This would have still given me some free time if my car had not broken down. The café is situated in a busy high street approximately ten minutes by car from my home. Parking is limited near this row of businesses and zealous traffic wardens regularly patrol here at all hours. The first few mornings I struggled to find a space to park to escort him to the door as he was daunted by the idea of walking in alone. Then, just as I felt able to drop him off, the travelling was about to become much more difficult. My car broke down and I was without it completely for some days as the garage waited for a spare part. Public transport to the area was available via two routes. The first involved regular buses but a significant walk to reach the venue. The second was direct but only ran half hourly at times which made us early or rushing to arrive breathless on time. We tried walking but the journey took about forty minutes and made him irritable. The planned simple journey had become complicated and long, relative to the two-hour slot. When I returned home, I barely had time to do anything before having to begin the return trip. I spent more time this fortnight at the nearby library and browsing in bookstores and charity shops than I had for years!

I had decided not to visit the café until his last day as I felt this would be best. However, on the last day I arranged to meet a friend there for lunch, thinking Ben would be proud to serve us. He did so but I could see that he struggled with me being there, as if my presence had brought together two separate worlds and he found that difficult to embrace.

Ben learned much from this experience. It increased his confidence around strangers, encouraged him to try new things, afforded him an insight into the workings of a café and gave him a penchant for hot chocolate! The staff helpers at the café were kind and thoughtful. They showed him how to work the hot drinks machine; explained how to do stocktaking and took him shopping to the suppliers in addition to the regular, basic tasks he completed. He learnt that most customers are kind and engaging but some are not. When he left, the staff gave him a signed card with their good wishes for his future and a box of chocolates. He was thrilled!

I was extremely grateful to them for this opportunity - a depth of gratitude that I had not experienced when his two brothers had done their work placements years before. I knew the debt was greater as the gift was more costly.

CHAPTER 34

Towards GCSE Science

The science department at Ben's comprehensive school struggled to understand his difficulties and accommodate them. One science teacher insisted that Ben should attempt a full GCSE paper at the age of thirteen so that she 'would afford him the same opportunity as every other child in his academic year'. I listened in disbelief to this justification for making him endure time spent under examination conditions with a paper he found impossible from beginning to end. She seemed insensible of the potential damage to self-esteem and futility of this activity and did not change her view even when I drew her attention to his low cognitive levels and his Statement of Needs. I expressed my disappointment to the school and tried to encourage my son.

The next year it was the formal a start to the GCSE course. I was both amused and furious to see the first homework set:

Learn how to spell the following:

protoctists, prokaryotes, unicellular, multicellular, saprophytically, autotrophically, heterotrophically, vertebrate, chordate

I mused on the fact that all other members of our family had gained top grades in GCSE science without using most of these words. I also noted that the move from simple explanations to technical scientific terminology in the intervening years severely prejudiced the chances of less able pupils whilst apparently gaining little for the high flyers.

After speaking to certain key individuals in the school hierarchy about some of these issues, changes were made. Some of the less able students were later spared the GCSE-for-all mock examination at thirteen and Ben's cohort followed alternative easier qualifications alongside the GCSE Science to avoid the possibility of total failure.

Despite my repeated requests for him to be withdrawn from GCSE science, Ben did eventually take the examination after a mock suggested that a G grade pass might be possible even if he did not pass all the written papers. Finally, we gave Ben the choice before reluctantly allowing him to be entered. We assured him that we only wanted him to try and were not concerned about the results. As the papers were of the multiple-choice variety, we simply suggested ticking one box at random if he did not know the answer. I was not sure that we had made the best decision.

His final science teachers deserve credit for their enthusiasm and for their diligence in offering a series of after-school revision sessions for the handful of lowest ability pupils. Ben attended most of these sessions, though his understanding and retention of the topics covered remained weak. To our surprise and his delight, he did obtain a low pass. For the science department, I am sure that their persistence with these weaker candidates had brought them a higher A-G pass rate, constantly stressed in the world of education in its mission to raise standards. Whilst I was pleased at one level, I still wondered if this was worth the time spent and the stress endured. As for scientific knowledge, Ben retains little, though he knows how to fill in multiple choice questionnaires, producing some interesting statistical data!

CHAPTER 35

Life at the Comprehensive School

After an unhappy start, Ben's secondary school career continued its course, at times sad and disappointing, at times happy and humdrum, punctuated by moments of triumph.

The first year included an assault on another pupil, much bullying, an exponential increase in aggression, much unhappiness, high levels of stress and a growing fear of what the future might hold.

At the end of this year, our social worker convened a meeting, which he chaired. It was attended by four representatives from the school, an educational psychologist, a representative from the LEA, a parent partnership representative and me. At this meeting my son's needs were discussed in detail. It was admitted that the transition from his previous school had not been not handled well. I admired the honesty of this admission. The social worker questioned whether the school was able to meet my son's needs. The LEA worker, who had played a key role in the decision to refuse a placement at the special school of our choice, sat passively in total silence. (I hoped she was now aware of the effect of her decision and perhaps willing to make different choices for those coming after us.) At the end of the meeting, it was agreed that I would investigate the possibility of a change of school for Ben to one of two special schools in the area. In the meantime, he was to remain on roll at his current school.

However, as this meeting took place in the last week of the summer term, this proved difficult to arrange and I was still in discussions with a possible school the week before the new term began in September. Then an unforeseen event occurred, which forced me to avert my attention to a more urgent matter: my mother-in-law suffered a massive haemorrhagic stroke. My husband and I spent a week at her side until her passing.

The timing of this tragic event meant that Ben returned to his school that September. We had other essential business to deal with for a few weeks and he settled back into his class. By the time we were able to reconsider the matter, we began to have doubts over the wisdom of moving him.

The school had put in place some key changes, including providing him with a learning assistant for his PE. Within a short while, he was engaging actively in the sporting life of the school, attending sports practices regularly at the end of the school day and for the next four years played football, table tennis and cricket in the school teams. This in turn gave him confidence and identity as he felt a real sense of achievement.

Celebration of achievement outside of the usual narrow academic focus was a fundamental ethos and strength of the school. Towards the end of year eight, the school held a special award evening, modelled on a graduation ceremony. The students were given degree grade certificates which they collected with a handshake from the head teacher, each one dressed in a mini graduation gown and mortar board. The ceremony was followed by a buffet prepared and served by hospitality students from the school. This was a fun occasion for everyone and a motivation booster for all students since the degree class was determined by points given for engagement in school life and attendance at school clubs and events, not for academic success. This meant that Ben and his peers could compete favourably with their more able counterparts. He will never attain a university degree but his photograph from this evening stands proudly alongside his brothers' graduation ones!

In year nine, he had a part in the chorus for the annual musical production. This involved attending many practices, culminating in a week of performances. The school provided a support worker for all these practices and backstage for the performances, which made it possible. Ben was very proud that he had done this, but not keen to repeat the experience in subsequent productions as he found it so demanding.

Sport was a key area where he could compete favourably with his peers and in his school career he gained colours in three sports, playing regularly in the school teams. In addition to the usual fixtures, he took part in annual table tennis tournaments, including a national final in London, best remembered by Ben for the trip to McDonald's on the way home! He also went to Lord's with the PE department to watch a cricket match and ended up having his photograph taken with Kevin Pietersen.

When he scored his first goal for the school, his PE teacher had a special certificate made for him, commemorating the exact moment it was scored. He was presented with it in assembly in front of his year group. As I had missed this moment by a few seconds, we were all keen for him to score again so that I could witness it. It was the last match of the season and the team were winning by a comfortable margin. Ben was on the pitch, playing up front. He had a fine shot but kept forgetting the rule and drifting into an off-side position, having played mainly 5-a-side all season. I was beginning to feel embarrassed as I could see his mistake being repeated. I was wondering how long it would be before he was taken off and replaced or made fun of by his peers. His teacher took the situation in hand and started shouting instructions to him telling him when to start his attacking runs. Knowing he could run fast, the teacher made a mental calculation of the time it would take Ben to reach the strike zone in time to play the ball without putting himself off-side. The strategy was employed a few times with near success. To my surprise and admiration, the young people on the touchline enthusiastically joined in, shouting their encouragement; it was as if the whole squad were willing Ben to score a goal.

'Now!' yelled the PE teacher at full volume. My son set off at full speed, and with exquisite timing, intersected the ball in a perfect position to draw back his left foot and rocket it home. The roar that went up was loud and genuine. Ben achieved his success, the team gained a digit on the scoreboard, the teacher was pleased and I got to witness my son scoring for the school team. It was as if everyone there had played a part in this little cameo and everyone shared that sense of satisfaction and pride. This was team work and integration at its best!

Finally, he went to a Chinese restaurant with the football squad at the end of his last year. As I dropped him off at the chosen restaurant, I felt a sense of immense pride. This was an occasion to celebrate not just the team's success but his inclusion within it, a triumph of acceptance and participation begun by his teacher but embraced by a group of teenagers. It showed what could be achieved with will and determination!

As Ben went through the teenage years and hormonal changes began to take effect, his moods became more dramatic and his behaviour more threatening. Although the worst of this took place at home, changes were noted at school and these developments were regularly discussed at our routine meetings with the psychiatrist. He raised serious concerns and convened a meeting of all parties to discuss Ben's case. This meeting was similar to the one called by the social worker two years earlier but the atmosphere was entirely different. This time the room was filled with individuals who knew Ben well, wanted the best for him and were willing to consider all possibilities to find the optimum solution. No one was there to defend their position, or to pursue their agenda and each one had personal knowledge of my son, obtained over an extended period of time. The proposal put forward by the psychiatrist, supported by the social worker, was for consideration of a move to a special needs school since they felt that the pressure of unrealistic expectations and homework might be contributing to his deteriorating behaviour. At the special school, homework was not given and life skills formed a significant part of the main curriculum. This seemed an appropriate solution, though I felt no real conviction that this was the answer.

As parents, we requested a staged move, with Ben attending both schools concurrently for a transition period. This we felt would give him less stress than leaving his friends and familiar environment suddenly. It would also give us the option to remain at his original school if things did not work out as expected. This idea was well-received and for a while, he was on dual roll - registered part time at both schools. We explained carefully to him what we proposed and he began his new schedule. At his insistence, we purchased school uniform for the new school as he did not want to be different. He coped well with his new routine enjoying cooking regularly and two sports days that summer. He also went to see the Olympic torch parade with his new school which particularly delighted him as his other school did not do so.

During the few months that followed, I had regular conversations with the staff at the new school and was even asked to consider becoming a parent governor. However, as time progressed it became apparent that Ben felt much more at home in his old environment. He struggled to make new friends and the other pupils who had spent several years together struggled to accept him. The life skills programme that he joined for was not significantly different from what his teachers had been providing informally. Only the stress of homework had been removed. At the Learning Resource Base changes had also been proposed for the following year and the member of staff set to take responsibility for years 10 and 11 was now the teacher who knew him best. After a few months, we unanimously agreed that he would revert to full attendance at his old school. His friends cheered. He was relieved. We had trialled the alternative. We had found it to have no real advantages. Everyone was happy, Ben most of all. We had definitely made the right decision. From here on, he settled down at school and enjoyed the remaining two years.

Ben's school days were spent mainly in the Learning Resource Base, a cluster of rooms, within the wider school but with its own identity and sense of community. The team running this learning base were inspirational, a band of dedicated teachers and assistants committed to going beyond the requirements of their contracts to give these young people the greatest opportunities possible within the confines that time, finance and the students' limitations allowed. The students spent most of their time within the unit but attended lessons with specialist teachers in different rooms around the main part of the school. They were also assigned to a tutor group and went with them to assemblies and daily registration periods. This kept them in touch with the wider school and its activities.

My son particularly enjoyed some of the more practical activities. He regularly attended the art club run by his art teacher who encouraged him to work on his basic creative skills. This gave him an opportunity to work at his coursework as well as make things related to seasonal events in the calendar. It was a feature in his week; he rarely missed a session.

He enjoyed the gardening project which involved the students clearing a large plot in a local community garden and growing a variety of vegetables and sunflowers there. Each member of the small group had their special jobs as well as contributing to the general effort when required. Ben was great at watering the sizeable plot in the dry summer months, carrying his big watering can from one end to the other, heavy with water from the outdoor tap, amazed at how much water the ground would devour. The students were very proud of their achievements, especially when harvesting came around. They were devastated too when some of their plants died, despite their best efforts. At the end of the gardening course, they invited the parents to visit the community garden, prepared cakes and drinks for us and showed us their handiwork. The head teacher circulated among them all, offering his congratulations and asking for their gardening tips. Finally, the students gathered for a Gardening Team photo before he presented them each with a certificate. Their pride in their visible achievements was evident to all.

At the end of Year 11, Ben was thrilled to go to the School Prom. It was a grand occasion, held in a well-known local venue. We bought him his first suit and tie for the event and he talked about it for weeks before and afterwards. At this event, he was given a special sash, as a recipient of an honorary award. On it was the words, 'human filofax', a reference, I believe to his encyclopaedic memory of birthday dates. It was a bit of fun and kindly meant and he revelled in the glory of it. Formal photographs were taken and a memorable evening was had by all.

At the end of term, he was asked to collect his record of achievement, including his exam passes to date. He had attained BTEC qualifications in Hospitality, PE, Art, Gardening, Maths, English and Science. To these would later be added the GCSE certificate in Science.

We were all proud of his achievements and conscious of the immense effort they represented which for another pupil might have resulted in high academic passes.

As he left this familiar environment for the last time, I felt a mixture of gratitude, nostalgia and a sense of parting, along with real concern about what the transition to college would bring. For Ben, whilst he was sorry to be leaving his friends, teachers and helpers behind, he drew a clear line between the future and the past which he placed in a neat labelled box in his memory. He did not go to that school now. He was going to college.

CHAPTER 36

The Bus Pass

I realised one day that if I never allowed Ben to go out alone, he would become totally dependent on adult support. I contemplated what he would forfeit if that were the case, the freedoms he would never have; the life he would never lead. Then I determined that I must at least try. I began to develop a strategic plan to steer him through the long, difficult path over uncharted terrain, to independence. I did not know whether he would ever reach the destination but I promised myself that I would assist him in the attempt. I calmly evaluated the facts, made calculations based on what I thought could be achieved in a given timescale. I prepared my risk assessment, knowing that his awareness of danger is greatly impaired, then mentally drew up a plan involving incremental steps towards the unseen summit. As with eager climbers, I began the training far below base camp, aware that altitude sickness, falls or bad weather could prevent the best-prepared trainees from achieving their goal. We were not close to being amongst the best-prepared!

The first step was to give him a front door key, to let himself into the house when driven home from school by taxi and escort. He seemed to like this, enjoying the new sense of freedom and independence. At first I was in the house, but gradually I began to ask him to let himself in when I was no longer in. At first, I returned shortly. I then increased the time he was left, aware that my phone number and his father's were left clearly visible next to the phone. He usually phoned me on entering the empty house, for the reassurance of my voice and for the unspoken commendation of what he had achieved. I began to have greater windows of time enabling me to work occasional afternoons.

Then the real training started. I began by dropping him off at the end of our residential road, a few hundred yards from our home. No roads to cross, no evident obstacles. I followed in the car, observing, stalking, hoping. Success. I began giving him one quiet side-road to cross, still following furtively in my car.

Confidence began to increase for both of us. I remember the first time I sent him to the corner shop bakery, grasping the exact money for an iced bun. I waited with an uneasy mix of fear and determination as he moved momentarily out of sight. He returned a few minutes later, with an agitated smile and a half-eaten bun!

We began to increase the gradient and distance of our practice tasks. I introduced him to the pelican crossing over the busy road near the end of our quiet, residential street. It was not the closest crossing to our house, but the safest and I always asked him to use it.

"You must always wait for the green man, even if other people walk across!"

'They have judgement that you do not have,' I thought to myself 'but what happens if the pedestrian lights fail? Then you would not cope.'

"If the lights do not work, you must ask an adult to help you cross or come back home!"

I always tried to foresee any problem because then I might be able to teach an appropriate response to it. I was aware that my capacity to foresee every possibility was limited therefore this strategy was inevitably flawed. I constantly reappraised my risk assessment. Total elimination of risk is never possible. My job consisted in reducing the level of risk. I sounded like an insurance underwriter with my projections and calculations but this had my son's life at stake. Whilst it became a strategy game, the risks were always real!

There was always an element of unpredictability in my son's behaviour. After I had begun to relax about him crossing familiar minor roads, I watched him walk home one day from a few streets away. The territory was totally familiar. He had one minor road to cross. There was only one logical route to my non-autistic mind. Then I watched in disbelief as instead of taking this path, he crossed one major road a few yards down from a Pelican crossing before crossing back a hundred yards further down. This avoided the minor road completely. Why? To me there seemed no possible reason. To him there surely was - perhaps to avoid a dog he knew lived near there, perhaps to avoid other pedestrians, perhaps? Whatever the reason, he had chosen to put himself in danger twice to change his route. Two steps forward, one large step back! There would always be that element of risk.

At around this time, it occurred to me that a future for Ben with any degree of independence would involve the use of public transport. Ben would never drive. He would never be rich. Buses and perhaps trains would be the only realistic means of local travel. It was a long time since he had even been on a bus. I began to take him out, showing him what to do, guiding him along the main route to the centre of town and talking him step by step through the process of going on a simple bus journey. The cost surprised me as fares had increased greatly since I had last used public transport. These expeditions were proving expensive, especially as they were only the means of getting somewhere, and to Ben, merely an adjunct to some more exciting adventure! I had been told that the local authority offered bus passes to children with disabilities and an escort. I decided it was time to apply for one.

Having checked out what was needed with the website, I gathered all my documentary evidence, including a signed form from my GP for which a ten-pound charge was applicable, which proved to be worthless in supporting our cause. I parked my car in the pay and display car park near the council offices and took my ticket at the counter queue. I was called and presented my supporting evidence. The clerk was friendly and positive, suggesting I take a seat while she dealt with the paperwork. I was grateful for the seat but left bemoaning my failure to bring a novel with me from my car. The wait lasted twenty-five minutes and apart from a brief consolatory conversation with a kindred soul, I was left bored, frustrated and regretting my lost time. Eventually my name was called and I sprang up, eager to retrieve my new bus pass and leave. She handed me a piece of paper with a few ticked boxes.

"Is this the bus pass?" I asked sceptically.

"Oh no, that will arrive in a few weeks' time by post. This is a receipt for you to say that we have photocopied the documents."

'So, I have waited twenty five minutes for you to photocopy a few documents?' The question was rhetorical and unspoken. The clerk seemed to have understood, however, and with a look of helpless apology, she attended to the next client.

A few days later, a letter arrived from the Transport section of the council stating that the evidence presented in support of our claim for a bus pass was inadequate. In particular, the GP letter stating that my son had learning difficulties and was on the autistic spectrum was inadequate proof that he needed the pass. The fact that it was stated in the same letter that my son needed support to go out and that we were hoping to gradually introduce him to public transport as a means of developing independence was apparently also inadequate for their criteria.

I was asked to provide one of the following types of evidence:

1) Evidence that he qualified for a government benefit related to mobility issues (which he did not have because his disabilities were not physical.)

2) Confirmation of registration with Social Care (This eventually proved the trump card!)

3) Proof of a special education provision (This criterion led me to engage in an interesting debate with a senior Council clerk.)

4) Medical evidence from a specialist or GP (I did not want to bother our consultant with this matter and the GP route had already proved futile.)

At the suggestion of my son's school, I decided to phone the council for clarification about what was acceptable proof. At first, my call was answered by a young man who assured me that if my son was physically able to walk, he would not qualify for a bus pass at all. I told him that this position was unreasonable as it discriminated between individuals with a physical disability and those with other kinds of impairment. I suggested it would be helpful if I could speak to his superior.

The first thing the supervisor did was to apologise for her colleague's ignorance of the system. They *did* offer bus passes for people with other disabilities, indeed they had a section related to this on their form, but the evidence I had offered was not specific enough to meet their strict criteria. I then asked her what sort of evidence would be admissible from my son's school. I suggested they might like to see his statement of special educational needs, a document of some fifteen or more pages, or a letter from the council confirming provision of escorted transport to and from school? The lady was quite happy to accept this information until she discovered that he attended a comprehensive school.

At the sound of the words 'mainstream school', she seemed to think that this would no longer be acceptable. I sighed loudly and shifted to campaign mode. I explained to her that although he had been offered a place at a special school, it was my right as a parent to send my child to a mainstream school if I chose; that inclusion in mainstream had formed a major thrust of government policy in education in the last three governments… In her defence, she cited her rule book of eligibility criteria, declaring that this was all she had by way of instructions.

Eventually, I asked her if a letter from a social worker would satisfy. She seemed to think it might. We finished our conversation there. I contacted my social worker. He was very helpful. He understood the situation. He had encountered such issues before with other clients. He agreed to write an email supporting our claim. Within half an hour, the email was written, the bus pass was approved for five years and my social worker emailed me to say that the pass would be arriving shortly.

When the pass arrived, I looked over it, a small plastic photo card, the size and shape of a credit card. In the top corner was a letter C with a plus sign. There was no mention of an escort being allowed to travel with the cardholder. On investigation, I was informed that the sign in the top corner meant that an escort could travel free of charge, in fact the holder could *only* travel with an escort.

"Oh," I sighed to myself, reminded yet again of the narrow vision of bureaucrats. "but the aim is for him to become independent. At that point, I would have to go through the application process all over again…"

CHAPTER 37

The Explicit Phone Call (Inappropriate Public Behaviour and Reactions to it)

Like many teenagers exploring new sensations and emotions, Ben's hands occasionally strayed into his underpants because he found this touch experience pleasant. We did not encourage this, quite the opposite in fact, but tried to do so with tact and understanding. Here was someone already struggling to comprehend basic social rules thrown into a whirlwind of new issues as hormonal changes took place in his body. His teachers at school spoke with us and we discussed consistent approaches between the home and school environments.

This topic seemed to evoke different levels of emotional response from different individuals. His art teacher clearly found this matter distasteful and called me behind one day to express her viewpoint. It was not a discussion; she merely wanted me to witness her ultimatum:

"Either this stops happening or you are no longer allowed to come to art club!"

Ben loved art club. He did not really understand why his teacher was so upset but he understood her simple statement and her disapproval. I repeated the words before we left to go home, adding, "It's your choice!" He continued to enjoy art club and the teacher never complained again.

The issue did not fully disappear either at home or in his main class but a look or a simple wave of the hand was all that was required to distract. It was a gentle touch sensation not a major sexual act and did not happen all the time. When we discussed it with Ben's psychiatrist, he did not seem surprised but advised us to concentrate on appropriate location and privacy.

So when we arranged for Ben to go on the National Citizenship Scheme for three weeks of activities, including two five-day residential periods, it never occurred to me that this problem could present itself. Nor could I ever have dreamed about the telephone conversation I was to have the day he had left for camp. It was late afternoon when the phone rang. It was from the camp organiser.

"Is that Ben's mother?"

"Yes - is he alright?" by now I was concerned for his welfare.

"There has been an incident."

He proceeded to tell me in a tone of veiled disgust that my son had been witnessed with his hand down his trousers, 'looking at the girls in the dinner queue'. I do not know whether this incident was merely a pair of straying hands or a major sexual incident. I only know that I spent the next interminable minutes discussing 'a sexual act' that I was neither involved in nor witness to, in graphic detail with a man I had never met, receiving the full brunt of his disdain and disapprobation until I felt myself to be unclean, tainted and despised.

Summoning all my dignity, I asked in a deceptively calm tone how they had dealt with this. He said they had removed him from the scene and told him this was not acceptable conduct. The group leaders had also approached the other young people in his cohort and asked them if they were willing for him to remain and to accept him with his additional needs. They had unanimously agreed to do so. I asked what he wanted me to do next and was informed that Ben could stay as long as the incident was not repeated.

I realised that this had been a reaction to extreme stress, that it was probably unrelated to the social interaction around him. I also realised that had I been the parent of another student in his group, I might have been unable to see this as alarm bells for social and sexual deviance and concern for my child would have drowned out these considerations.

The phone calls I had made explaining his special needs and the unheeded request for a support worker for him on this trip flashed across my memory. The recurring theme in my head was how the words 'all-inclusive' usually expressed desire rather than expertise in accommodating all needs. It was as if following legal requirements or attending training courses actually equipped you for the real thing. I had attended plenty of courses and I had faced real issues - I knew the gulf between the two. I also knew that until you faced the real, the training manuals looked so comprehensive.

I wanted to give Ben a hug and talk to him about how he felt now. I asked to speak to him. The organiser said he would go and fetch him, leaving me waiting, wondering how the next few days would work out.

In our conversation that followed, I trod a delicate path between expressing love and acceptance and making him aware of the need to avoid repetition of this event. Ben, whilst aware he had been chastised, was clearly unaware of the social implications of his actions or the gravity of the leader's reaction. When asked if he was willing to stay that night, he said he was. We told him that he could ask to speak to us or his brother at any time and that we would collect him if he did not want to continue. We also promised that one of us would speak to him every night whilst he was away.

Initially, I only spoke to two individuals about this incident besides my husband and the son who was soon to be responsible for him during our forthcoming absence. The first was the mother of two children with special needs; the second a nurse. They reassured me, expressed surprise at the degree of fuss over the incident and felt that amongst disabled teenagers this issue was commonplace. I then felt it my duty to speak to the church youth leader and the person in charge of the college course he was soon to attend. They were matter of fact, understanding and unruffled. I felt relieved.

Somehow he did make it through to the end of the scheme, even completing the night hike which he hated but was proud he had completed. When we attended the certificate presentation event some months later it was clear that the other young people were proud of him too and had learnt much from having him there. The helpers seemed genuinely pleased that they had steered Ben to a positive ending, after such a shaky start. Fortunately for me, there were many organisers and though we thanked various individuals, I never had to look in the eyes of the voice I had spoken to on the phone that day - I was grateful for being spared that moment.

CHAPTER 38

Shingles, Shouting and Running Dry

We had been on holiday for a few days with my eighty-two-year-old mother, staying in a village in the Welsh countryside. It had one garage shop and a café but no chemist and no doctor's surgery. The nearest town was some fifteen minutes' drive away. I had already spent seven hours in the nearest accident and emergency department, about twenty miles further West, after my mother fell and fractured her arm.

Ben had been complaining for several days about his rash. In a combination of "It itches," and "It hurts." I was finding it hard to work out quite how bad it really was. It did look angry and rather unusual. The skin was raised and red. We applied a soothing cream which reduced the redness without dealing with the cause. For a couple of days we talked about seeking advice from a chemist or trying to make an appointment with a local GP but Ben was happy to continue with the day trips we had planned and somehow it did not seem to be a priority.

On the day we left, Ben was still complaining. He had enjoyed the few days away but did not like the upheaval and exertion of packing up and carrying bags and boxes to the car. When it was finished, he climbed into the front seat next to my husband and they turned on the CD player at high volume. My mother and I, sitting in the back near the speakers received the full sound at close proximity. For a while, nothing was said but eventually I asked if we could have a break from the constant sound. Ben was not happy. I approached the issue from a reasoned standpoint. My mother and I had listened to music during every car journey over the last few days, perhaps it was time for us to have our choice of a break, just for a short while.

Within minutes, Ben began to perseverate, both about the music and his rash. We had a two-hour car journey ahead of us but as the day was warm and sunny, we had decided to break it up with a stop at a beach on the way. We nearly made it to the beach but Ben's agitation reached boiling point about half a mile from our destination. Confined in a small space on a narrow country road, trying to shield my mother from the worst, with Ben about to explode, was not a good place to be! Eventually, Richard and I knew we had to stop.

He brought the car to a halt on the verge near an isolated row of farm cottages and the two of them disappeared out of sight into a wooded area behind. The place was deserted and apart from an occasional car on the winding road, my mother and I saw no-one. There was no place to sit. There was nowhere to go. The only thing to do was to wait. At first there was not much said between us as we contemplated the details of our surroundings. One thought that occurred to both of us was that anyone wishing to drive away from the cottages would find it difficult to pass us. My mother asked if I would move our car if required, then I realised that I did not even have a key. A long time passed. We had no idea where they were or whether Ben was now calmer. I walked to a vantage point but could see nothing except an empty path disappearing into a wood. Then I remembered that Richard had his phone with him. We briefly exchanged texts:

13.34 Everything OK?

13.34 Yes.

13.39 Taking a time.

13.40 Anything we can do?

13.41 No

14.03 Any news?

So we had to wait. In between the silences, my mother and I shared our concerns for the future. Eventually they returned. Ben was still agitated but slightly less so than when they had left. We continued on to the beach in an uneasy silence, aware that things could rapidly deteriorate. After a few twists and turns, we came to a signpost for the beach. We had our picnic, a game of beach tennis and then a quick dip. After the tennis, Ben's mood seemed to be improving and continued to do so for the rest of the day. We made it back to my mother's house, tired, wary of upsetting Ben again but without further incident.

That night I had a rare altercation with my mother. She was weary and in pain from her broken arm. I was disappointed because she knew I was drained yet she still seemed to require more of me. I flipped and shouted at her. It was as if too many people needed me that night and I had nothing more to give. I do not regret what I said. It was not unreasonable. I regret raising my voice to her to say it. She was upset. I was exhausted. I sent Richard to check that she was ok and retreated to my bed. Tomorrow would be another day. Tomorrow I would have new love to give, today I needed to sleep!

The next morning mum and I greeted each other with a lengthy hug and an apology and resumed our close relationship.

A few days later when we finally had a chance for Ben to see our GP, we were told he had shingles. 'So it *had* hurt, it *was* unpleasant and he *had* probably felt unwell for the last few days. There was a reason for this outburst after all.' I felt sad. I felt like a bad mother. Then I realised that sometimes you get things wrong but your best is all you have, even if it falls short. So I gave my son the kind of hug that says 'I am sorry I let you down but I will always love you, please forgive me!' But I knew that in his childlike way, he already had.

CHAPTER 39

The Talent Show

When Ben came home one evening with the announcement that some girls from his youth club were organising a talent show I was less than enthusiastic, especially when he told me he had already volunteered to sing a solo. I do not like these events. I do not have a solo singing voice and would hate the opportunity to be on the stage with a microphone and a backing track. I have sordid memories of listening to others try at talent shows and karaoke evenings and being embarrassed at their misplaced confidence in their limited ability. So from this prejudicial standpoint my first thought was to try and dissuade Ben from his idea. I gently suggested that he did not have to sing, that plenty of others might want to do so. I secretly hoped we might have something on that night and checked my calendar to see. The page was blank. I had no excuse. The youth leader also spoke to Ben assuring him that he could change his mind if he wanted to. He did not.

A few weeks before, Ben was listening to a music video on You Tube, as he often did, singing happily over the track. He informed me he had decided the song he wanted to perform and he was practising. He did so frequently over the next couple of weeks. His voice was strong and singing over the recording, his timing and pitch were good. I was still worried that on the night, with an audience and only the music accompaniment, his voice might become thin or lose its pitch.

On the day of the show, Richard took him to the afternoon rehearsal and I joined them in time for the start of the event. Unlike some of the performers who had dressed up for the occasion, Ben wore a simple T-shirt and his only pair of jeans. It did not matter and I did not want to upset him in any way by suggesting a change. He was happy.

Richard and I sat with a friend at one of the informal tables arranged around the large hall. It was nearly full and there was an expectant buzz as we waited for the programme to begin. The first performer was a young man in his twenties who gave a fine rendition of a well-known song. Other acts followed of a similar high standard. Some of these soloists were clearly used to being on stage in front of an audience. There was an interval when drinks and cupcakes were served. Still Ben had yet to perform. He sat with his friends on the other side of the room, waving occasionally and seemed to be enjoying the proceedings. Then I saw the organiser have a brief word with him between acts and I knew his turn was soon. As Ben got up from his seat he looked over to us for a brief moment of reassurance before taking the stage. He fidgeted while the intro played and I held my breath, bracing myself. Then he began to sing. His performance was stunning and I felt chastened as he held the audience enthralled. As the last note was sung, everyone rose to their feet, thrilled *for* him and *with* him. Ben's face was radiant as he revelled in the applause before taking his seat. I exhaled deeply. Well done Ben!

At the end of the evening, Ben was invited to do an encore, the only performer to do so. It was *his* night! As I left the building, a friend commented:

"What about your Ben, the star of the show!"

I felt so proud. How could I have ever doubted?

CHAPTER 40

The Church

My Christian faith is very important to me and I know God has sustained me in the most difficult moments. We have been at our current church for over thirty years and my church family is like an extension of my own. My children have grown up in this wider family and Ben has loved the worship and the camaraderie of the church ever since he overcame his reticence at the loud music that forms part of our Sunday services. Both Richard and I engage in expressive dance in the worship times using coloured banners and gymnastic ribbons. Ben, having a good natural sense of rhythm also enjoyed dancing with flags until he joined with the teenagers in sitting on the balcony at the age of fourteen. It was the thing to do.

Despite the closeness of our church family, few in the church really know and understand the issues that we face. Those who do have been very supportive although few know practically what to do to help. One family regularly invite Ben over, including him in family activities with their younger children. He loves this and they have fun together. Ben enjoys church family life and is good at playing with younger children.

Two ladies have babysat for us for special events, enabling us to attend family and work events and go out occasionally. Several others pray for us, including a small team who met regularly when things were particularly difficult; I know this has made a difference. Some admire us and think mistakenly that we can cope with anything. The majority have no idea, particularly since our son always seems calm at church.

The youth leader has a wonderful relationship with Ben. He understands him, brings out the best in him and leads others into doing likewise. He is always a calming influence, never condescending and very patient. He has taken Ben away on several camping trips with the young people. We trust him and so does Ben. This has enabled us to take short breaks when he is away. It has made a big difference to our lives and to Ben's.

The young people of the church accept my son as part of the wider group. Their attitude is not always perfect (they are teenagers, after all), but most of the time they accept the quirkiness that Ben displays and enjoy playing table tennis, dodgeball and football with him. Occasionally he irritates them and he can be left on the fringe of social interaction. Mostly they embrace him in the atmosphere of acceptance modelled by Jesus in the New Testament on which we try as a church to base our lives.

Ben never misses the weekly activities that he enjoys and is one of the few who regularly join in with local inter-church youth events held in different churches in the area. He loves the openness of these occasions and the safe environment where he can meet new people and do things together.

When Ben was fifteen, the youth leader started up a church football team with weekly practices and fixtures in a local league. At first I was doubtful whether he would cope without the safety net of tolerance that is integral to his disability club. I suggested that he tried it out for a while to see if he liked it. Once again, sport proved a great leveller for him, especially when he volunteered to go in goal when their usual goalie was unavailable, a position that most of the boys did not like. As Ben demonstrated his various skills and versatility, he became respected as a key member of the squad. They were proud to reach the league cup final when most parents and the church leader turned out to support, but saddened to lose it despite trying hard. Looking back they had enjoyed the season with its usual mixture of triumph, frustration, activity, camaraderie and fun!

As Ben progressed through his teens, he began to help in the church café. Before the age of sixteen, he was allowed to wait on tables but not enter the kitchen area. His sense of achievement and pride was evident even in the simplest of tasks achieved. It was a tentative first step into the world of work but a major milestone for him. He continued to work occasional days in the cafe in his school holidays and when he left school at sixteen, he worked for a few days each week before starting college. The atmosphere of acceptance there was amazing amongst both the customers and the staff and he loved it. The lady in charge told him he could help there whenever he could and he does.

Recently the young people organised a talent show to raise money for a church building project. It was planned and run by teenagers with a mixture of young people, youth workers and friends performing in the programme. Ben immediately volunteered to sing, keen to be involved in the project, to play his part. He did so, exceeding everyone's expectations.

One day, my son came home and asked to be baptised. I was reluctant to rush in to this at first, fearing it might be a 'copycat' decision. I battled too with the authenticity of his faith in the light of the aggression and wildness that I sometimes see in him. After a while and several repeated requests, we let the church leaders decide. He met with the youth leader and a decision was made. He was baptised in the church one Sunday morning and even spoke a few brief sentences about his decision to take this step. His brothers and his grandmother attended the service especially for the occasion. He was very proud. I believe his faith is genuine though his understanding remains limited. I am glad we allowed him to be baptised. God's love is unconditional: He does not penalise us for lack of understanding!

PART 4

Reflections

CHAPTER 41

Forms, Meetings and Red Tape

At one of the first events I attended for parents of children with disabilities, I met a mother whose child was several years older than my own. She cared deeply about her child but her tone was weary, disillusioned and pugilistic.

"I used to go into meetings asking politely for things for my son, now I just walk in and demand what I need."

Her harsh tone jarred and saddened me and I confess a quiet sense of disapprobation at her brashness. Surely there was a more gracious approach to the issues? Now, several years on, I have tried not to adopt that tone, but fully understand the exasperation and despair that led her there.

In order to obtain support and due attention for a disabled child, it is necessary to fill in lengthy forms, asking specific personal information about the individual, your family, your finances and your daily routine. Some of the information for analysis is impossible to answer accurately:

Does the child need help understanding other people?

>   *Tell us about the child's difficulties understanding other people...*

>   *How many times a day do they need someone to help them understand other people?'*

>   *Tell us roughly how long it takes each time. (Please try to tell us in minutes.)*

Does the child need help being understood by other people?

>   *Tell us about the child's difficulties being understood by other people...*

>   *How many times a day do they need help to make themselves understood by other people?*

>   *Tell us roughly how long it takes each time?*
>   *(Please try to tell us in minutes)[2]*

Similar information can be expressed differently, with different outcomes. Often they require quantitative data where qualitative data is the only answer that would make sense. I realise that these bureaucratic machines have to differentiate the genuine from the false but it seems to me that whilst a few individuals can extort much from the system, many desperately needy families are deterred from starting the process and many more of us find the process distressing and intrusive. Most parents I have met share my dread of the twenty-eight page form which we are

---

2   DLA1 Child Form DWP

required to fill out, at regular intervals. Many have confessed to shedding tears as they fill out pages of information about all the difficulties they face with their children, difficulties they spend their lives dealing with but trying to forget.

Some parents never find out what help could be available to them. I might have been one of these but for a thoughtful lady who mentioned it whilst showing me around a special school in our area when Ben was still a toddler. I never saw that individual or visited that school again but I am grateful for the information she gave me. It has made a real difference to our family life in the years that have followed.

Then there are the endless rounds of meetings: medical, educational, educational psychologist and social work appointments and sometimes grand round table events with all assembled to discuss your child. All this comes in addition to the parents' evenings, social events and transport issues that all parents have to face. Full-time employment is rarely an option - few employers can indefinitely accommodate leave of absence on this scale.

The closest I came to breaking point was approaching the change between child and adult care. I spent twelve weeks completing forms and attending meetings. The two most important applications for financial support had a combined length of around eighty pages. I was ground down by the banality of bureaucracy until I felt my identity reduced to the signature at the end of a form and the required representation at an essential meeting. For three months after this I refused to complete a single form: it was my version of rehab.

At the beginning of this time I had been invited to a meeting where the declaration was made to assembled parents that Social Services, Healthcare Providers and Education Departments would share information which would make life easier for everyone and promote a holistic approach to young adult care. As we left the room, another mother and I exchanged comments expressing our scepticism. Silently, I rebuked myself for my cynicism and tried to be positive. Days later, I attended my first meeting with one of the three agencies. I alluded to the promise recently given. The individual looked away embarrassed and apologised, saying this had not happened yet; they all required their own paperwork. It was hard not to succumb to the thought that the previous encounter had merely added to the busy round of meetings, without offering hope for change.

The effort involved is worth it; there is help out there, from government agencies and from voluntary groups. The government offers financial and some practical support but of at least equal value are the services provided by voluntary groups. They help you discover that you are not alone, that others have similar or worse situations to deal with and that people exist who really understand how you feel because they have been there. This lessens the isolation by bridging the gulf through shared experience, helping you to feel part of something other than your personal, exclusive world, a reminder of life before this began.

CHAPTER 42

Lasting Impressions and Hasty Judgements

The first time I visited this small school, tucked away in an area of town I rarely frequented, I left shocked, sure that this was not appropriate for my quiet, polite son. The school was in the middle of a major refurbishment programme, with builders in abundance and temporary partitions in place throughout much of the main building. I tried to see through the chaos, to judge beyond the physical environment. The staff members were kind, welcoming, proud to show off their school, proud of its future plans, what they hoped it would become.

I was escorted around the complex and shown classes in action: a cooking session which was clearly enjoyed by all concerned; a woodwork lesson, with pleasure less obvious but a clear sense of achievement evident; a science lesson with striking 3D visuals for demonstrating the structure of cells, taking place in a cramped space. I observed lessons in Maths, English, Social Skills and viewed the playground surrounded by a high fence, closely resembling a prison yard. I was introduced to a speech and language expert who gave additional help to some pupils; shown a music room full of interesting and exotic instruments and taken through the dining area, which doubled up as the assembly hall. I saw both sad and happy children, from those with quiet, withdrawn characters to those exploding with life and ideas.

As I moved around the school, I observed that every internal door was locked, opened by my escort with a tag key strapped to her wrist. The gesture was instinctive, routine but I felt a deepening sense of incarceration as I realised that pupils did not enjoy freedom of movement around the school. This only increased when we passed a small windowless room, empty of furniture with a CCTV camera attached high on one wall.

"What's that room used for?"

"That's the cooling off room; a safe place where we send pupils to calm down. They are observed from the office by CCTV link. Fortunately, we do not have to use it often."

"A cell," I thought. I felt trapped, offended, shocked. My sense of imprisonment haunted me. I could not imagine this place ever being appropriate for Ben.

My final vision of this visit was to haunt me for a long time. As we crossed the path between buildings, I witnessed something I never wished to see; two teachers restraining a violent teenager who was kicking, screaming, swearing and threatening everyone. They dealt with him in a manner that was both professional and degrading, using current restraint guidelines. What I witnessed was the dehumanising of an individual, firstly by his own behaviour but secondly by measures employed to safeguard him and those around him. It was ugly, alarming and unforgettable. I thanked the staff for their time and left, believing I would never return.

Two years later, I sat in the head teacher's office, apologising for my hasty judgement. I explained that my son's conduct had changed so much in the intervening time that I could now understand the need for many of the measures in place in her school. I told her that I was now reviewing the options available to him as we considered a change of placement. She was understanding, kind and gave generously of her time. She did not judge. She did not attempt to influence my decision. I respected her professionalism and compassion.

My son never attended this school fully, though he spent a number of individual days there as we tried to make an informed decision about his school environment. Our decision for him to remain at his original placement was not based on the unsuitability of this provision, rather on the advantages of familiarity and stability. The staff at this school work tirelessly for their pupils, with limited support from parents and the local community but with infinite enthusiasm and courage. The devices employed by them to maintain safety in their school environment are affected as unobtrusively as possible in the context of affirming the value of each individual. Intervention such as I witnessed is rarely employed. I just happened to witness it that day. Once again I came to realise how easy it is to form hasty judgements which do not always stand the test of time.

CHAPTER 43

Coffee Tables and Riding Lessons

Sometimes I assume a lifestyle which appears like everyone else's. I have moments of happy, experiences with my child for extended periods of time and we start to live as though autism has been removed from our lives. In one recent school holiday week, I had enjoyed a long walk, off the beaten track, in the woods, alone with Ben, chatting and feeling safe in his company. Another afternoon we had been swimming together in our local pool, racing lengths and playing ball in a familiar world. Later that week, I found myself shut in my husband's study to escape the fury and threats of violence, while my husband talked Ben down, in a flare-up caused by a single comment about the need for safeguarding in social media, intended to protect my vulnerable son, received by him as an invasion of privacy and an insult.

I never cease to be surprised by these moments. It seems as if my brain defaults to a state of low security risk, as if I cannot always live on red alert. This leads inevitably to being caught out, being disappointed but also gives us moments of experience common to the rest of society.

I recently purchased a new coffee table for my lounge. We had been looking for a while to replace a battered old one which we had used for years but never liked. It did not occur to me to discuss this with my son. Why should it? We brought the table home and swapped them over. It was rectangular in contrast to the old square table but its appointed place was the same - in the centre of the room, between the television and the sofa. Ben was uneasy from the moment it arrived, particularly when I stated clearly that I wanted the top reserved for an ornament and lace cloth, with a few coasters.

"Please keep the surface free of other things and do not put drinks on the table without using the coasters!" I said as I laid down house rules.

In practice, this meant that his laptop had to be accommodated somewhere else. I found a small table to begin with and placed it with the computer on it in the corner of the room. Ben looked at me doubtfully. I decided I was not going to give in. It was malaise, not meltdown and we all struggled through it.

What I was dreading telling him was that we had also bought a new suite which was arriving two days later. Eventually I plucked up the courage to do so and he looked confused but not annoyed. When Ben arrived home from college to find the new furniture in place, he took one look at it and continued with his normal routine. It was then that I realised that the table had bothered him because it affected him *personally* - he had needed to move his laptop to a new location. The new suite did not concern him because it simply replaced the old one, in exactly the same position. He could sit in it and watch television just as before, so it barely registered on his scale of difference, far less on his scale of offence.

The problem is working out whether aspects of change are going to cause anxiety or not and the degree of reaction from minor fizz to nuclear explosion. If I struggle to understand this, I suppose I cannot expect strangers to comprehend. Yet life is so much easier when people try…

Ben had been horse-riding for over a year when I began to find that the organisers were frequently giving him different horses from his stated choice. It was not as if he always asked for the same horse; we understood that they were keen for him to try riding different animals. Perhaps it was simply convenient to them to change at the last minute but to Ben it was an irritation. He was still coping quite well despite this when I arrived at the office one day to book the next lesson.

"We are changing the lesson times. Your son must change to a different day, with a new group and may have a change of teacher."

I sighed silently, thinking how difficult it would be for my son to accept three different changes at once. I tried to explain, reminding them of his diagnosis.

I was totally unprepared for the response:

"We are not a disabled riding school. We cannot treat him differently. Your son has to be treated like everyone else."

Whilst I understood the truth of her remark, the frustration of her day gave voice to a tone that was brutal and unfeeling. This was another of those moments when I felt felled on the inside. I was warring between the options of tears or shouting words in bitterness and anger that I might later regret. *I felt betrayed, betrayed by people I thought were on my side*. I had always found the staff there helpful and sympathetic but all this seemed false and unreal now.

221

"All I am asking for is a little humanity and consideration," I delivered with the stare of a trapped, wounded animal before walking out of the office to preserve my dignity. I was not going to allow her to witness my lost composure. Once outside, I cried - visibly but quietly, whilst inside my body heaved with great sobs of hurt and frustration. I knew Ben would not understand why I felt so offended. I knew he would not like the changes. I knew he enjoyed riding. At that moment, it was difficult to see an answer which would address all these issues.

I spoke to his teacher at the end of his lesson, conveying to her my feelings of offence and disappointment. She had always been kind to Ben. I could tell she did not share the sentiment her colleague had just expressed. She explained that they were all feeling very unsettled as major changes were taking place. She said that two teachers were leaving, including one who had resigned his post that day. I decided to pay for the lesson that had just finished but not book any more to give me time to consider what to do. She said she hoped we would return. I knew she would be happy to teach him.

I steered myself to a place of composure to drive home. Ben was confused. I was furious, disappointed, hurt but aware that he would not understand if I said I never wanted to return. We arrived home safely. It was several days before I reached a state of equilibrium.

Some weeks later, we tried out the new class, with the new teacher, on a different day. Ben did not enjoy it. He was restless and uneasy. He did not wish to go back unless he could have his old teacher. We decided to leave it until we could attend a class she taught. For now, it would not work with our other commitments. Riding would have to wait.

CHAPTER 44

Christmas and the Family

Christmas in our home is a Christian festival. It is also a celebration of family. It is a time when family members convene from their different places and lives to celebrate that sense of belonging and togetherness. It has always been so and when the children were younger, we would often make the long journey to cram into my parents' home to share the festivities together, joined by wider family groups at different points over the holiday period.

It was on one of these occasions that Ben's different view of proceedings became apparent. He had woken up first as usual and settled in front of the family television set to view his pick of children's programmes on Christmas morning. He was happy to wait to open presents until the remainder of the household stirred, which he figured could be some time since his older brothers, in their teenage years, though keen to stay up late, rarely appeared early in the holidays. As it was Christmas morning, one of his brothers had made a real effort to be sociable and entered the lounge, smiling, wishing all a 'Happy Christmas' and eager to open the presents together. Ben became agitated, rude and antagonistic.

To him, Christmas meant Jesus' birthday which we celebrated with a cake, birthday candles and, on occasions, a happy birthday chorus. It meant we spent time with each other, ate a special lunch together and had presents. Beyond this, to Ben, Christmas was a time when all sorts of things were inexplicably different. The shops, sports centres and swimming pools shut for several days. Television schedules were different. Mealtimes were altered. Decorations were everywhere. His football club had no matches or practices. His youth club had a few weeks off. Even cinemas shut. The usual familiarity of routine was suspended without explanation.

Ben did not like his brother getting up early. To him, this was an intrusion. He became agitated. I looked on with great sadness as I ushered my other son away from the room. I was overwhelmed by a sense of wrong. My middle son's enjoyment of the festivities should not be destroyed by his younger brother's attitude. In that moment, I wondered if these attitudes might one day drive our family apart. Would my children reach the point where they did not want to be together because doing so was so difficult? Little was said but the unspoken reassurance of my teenager, compassionate and wise beyond his years, told me that he understood. The presents were opened a little later. The day passed.

After this incident, Christmas at our house has become a crafted affair, a carefully orchestrated blend of keeping Ben busy whilst allowing his two brothers to enjoy a sense of relaxation and the freedom to chill out in their family home. We talk in advance about what will happen so as to minimise the unforeseen, unwanted surprises that could destroy the coveted peace of the season for all of us and try to relax whilst holding this intricate structure in equilibrium. Peace on Earth! Happy Christmas!

In his early teens, I had to sit Ben down and explain the myth of Father Christmas. It did not bother him though he found it all rather confusing. We still leave Father Christmas a drink and mince pie and his reindeer a carrot just as we have always done, simply out of tradition.

Ben now has recollections of previous years' proceedings so he knows it will pass but he still finds it strange that everything shuts down for an extended period and is often edgy. He enjoys the abundance of chocolate and party food in December and the chance to write his present list early in the autumn. As his birthday is in the spring, he understands that things which do not arrive in December may well arrive for his birthday.

When Ben was younger we used to take him to see some of the houses in our area festooned with Christmas lights. We still enjoy seeing the Christmas lights but do not make regular detours to find them as we once did. He is happy to put up our own tree early in December but keen to dismantle it as soon as the day is over; he cannot see why you might still want a Christmas tree up in early January!

Our family still meets together, though we rarely meet at Christmas with the wider groups. We have decided not to travel many miles on cold grey nights on crowded motorways to do so. We see relatives at different times; some often, others when busy schedules permit. Ben always looks forward to seeing them when it can be arranged.

CHAPTER 45

Talking v Conversation

Talking involves forming a recognisable pattern of sounds with coherent meaning which can be decoded by another individual. Conversation involves speaking, listening, turn-taking, reciprocal interaction and response.

Unlike many autistic individuals, Ben is sociable and extremely good at talking. He is particularly good at meeting people where intercourse is predictable and consistent and enjoys greeting old and new faces at our busy church services. He has an amazing memory for names, birthdays and people's interests and is willing to start a conversation with anyone. Ben is not so adept at reciprocal conversation, waiting for gaps to insert a response, listening or developing lines of argument or enquiry though he tries hard and achieves some success. He also understands considerably less language than he uses since he is a great mimic and often employs a bank of familiar phrases and ideas.

At home, we can find ourselves on the receiving end of one-way conversations, repeated narrative or questions, and tangential interruptions. This can make interaction strained and difficult when we try to steer the conversation instead of letting Ben do so. We use verbal cues and gestures to indicate that we are talking to each other rather than to Ben, to avoid confusion but longer conversations between other family members usually take place when he is busy.

Most days I try and sit with Ben to watch his favourite soap so that I am able to chat about the characters and events with him. He also enjoys watching quiz programmes with us. Although he cannot usually answer the questions, I think he enjoys the predictability of these shows and the banter between quiz masters and contestants. As a family, we sit down to our meals together and discuss the day's events or plans as well as items of sporting interest or news. Ben always enjoys this.

Ben loves to talk at length, sometimes with little space for me to reply. As a lover of silent old-fashioned libraries, the sounds of the natural world and gentle soothing music I can find this invasion of audible space difficult. I jealously guard my peace and sometimes have to retreat in solitude to find it. At these moments, my recurring dream is of a desert island where I am alone with nature, free to enjoy the silence, broken only by the soothing sound of the sea...

CHAPTER 46

Discipline

We knew a bit about discipline. We had two older children and we were both teachers. We knew it was important, that children need boundaries, that praise is often more effective than punishment but that punitive measures are sometimes needed. The problem was that with Ben nothing worked. In fact, any kind of sanction we could think of made the situation worse. It did not change his behaviour but it made him more aggressive and his reactions wilder. This made our lives more difficult, our ground less secure. We tried withholding Ben's access to computer games, television programs, mobile phone and *Facebook*; encouraging him to go to his room to take time out or removing him from stressful situations. We followed the usual guidelines: be fair, give positive reinforcement for good behaviour; have reasonable expectations, all for limited effect. The only strategy that reduced the tension was to avoid anything likely to cause him stress.

We utterly failed to eliminate occasional meltdowns. Once these had occurred, the only route that led eventually back to some degree of calm consisted of Richard spending hours alone with him talking him down, often having banished me from sight because it meant I was safe and it irritated Ben less. It was not practical. It was not convenient or acceptable. It was distressing and time-consuming but it was the only route down from the cliff top so sometimes we had to suspend whatever we were doing and use the single system that worked.

Distraction was effective if Ben's anger had not reached a critical point and occasionally if it had, like the time I called in my neighbour one evening when Ben was in full flight. I did so for my protection until Richard could respond to my SOS call and drive the ten-minute journey home from a friend's house. As soon as Ben saw my neighbour, a large rugby-playing sports teacher, his brain flipped into a different mode. He began to chat happily about Chelsea Football Club, an interest they shared. Ten minutes later as my husband arrived, the crisis was long passed and we were all left wondering why the visitor was there!

CHAPTER 47

Numbers, Time and Experience (Finding Constants)

Ben does not seem to have made much progress in maths since the age of about six or seven. You naturally assume that slow progress will be made. It comes as a shock to realise that the problems he works at today are pretty much the same as those he struggled with ten or more years ago. Education, even good education, cannot take individuals beyond their natural capacity to learn, however much enthusiasm, different methods and examples you bring. Repetition does not guarantee progress.

Breakthroughs are made, only to find that this new level of skill cannot be reliably replicated. Ten pence could have the same value as ten pounds or one hundred pounds; an hour could be the same as three; a week as long as a month or two.

This has the effect of altering the gravitational pull of life. The world is not as others know it; the Earth's axis no longer tilts at 23.4

degrees. Value is a foundational element in our society. Remove it and society's order collapses into a shadow of its former self.

Time is a compound substance comprising division of passing between day and night, awareness of present, past, future; consciousness of punctuality and lateness and appreciation of history. The concept of each of these is altered in a world where numerical value has no constants. I cannot imagine how it must be to live in that world. I know, however, that the 23.4 degree tilt gives a constancy, predictability and stability that some inhabitants of this planet cannot share: their source of these fundamental securities must be derived elsewhere.

For many such individuals, stability is derived from learned predictability. If you press the button and wait, the pedestrian light will turn green; if you turn on the television when you arrive home from school, this programme will be on; if you buy milk from a shop, it will taste fresh... this value system only operates effectively for predictive scenarios. If something changes, the system collapses. What do you do if the traffic lights do not function, the bus does not come or someone tells you to cross when the lights are red? Your world has lost its form. There is no structure. Without past experience, you have no basis for logical decision making. Life is chaotic and confusing. This is the world that my son inhabits.

On the positive side, a value system based on prediction becomes more effective if a regular pattern of activity is repeated, thus Christmas Day is now less stressful than it once was for Ben because he has memories of what happened in previous years. Unfortunately, you cannot predict every circumstance, but this helps for many everyday scenarios. It may be flawed but it provides some order in the chaos.

CHAPTER 48

Laughter

Laughter is an expression of human emotion. It is a mechanical process. It is easy to recognise and quantify. Humour, by contrast, is very difficult to define. It requires empathy, understanding and contextualisation. Ben has an acute deficit of these yet when he was younger he laughed more than anyone I know and he continued laughing long after everyone else had stopped. He laughed when others laughed, he laughed in response to my stress; he laughed to fill the silence and to gain attention. He laughed most frequently when he did not know what to do.

"Please don't laugh. I could be dead on the pavement and you would be there laughing."

"This is not the right time to laugh. That is a serious car accident. The man on the road is badly hurt. He may even die. The police and ambulance are helping him to get to hospital. Do you understand?"

"Yes - sorry mum, I won't laugh next time."

I was doubtful about his ability to do this, not because he wanted to be disrespectful but because the origin of his laughter was different. I silently prayed he would never be the first on the scene at an accident.

At one time, he would laugh when someone cut their finger or grazed their knee. We have stressed the need to wash a cut and fetch a plaster and some progress has been made. It is easier for him to know how to react if he knows *what he should do*. We have encouraged him to get help if he does not know. Whether he would respond appropriately at a time of crisis, remains in doubt.

Despite his limitations, Ben does enjoy some comedy programmes such as *Dad's Army* where the humour is often both predictable and visual.

I sometimes wonder how debilitating it must be to have such a limited appreciation of humour and whether laughter without it has the same therapeutic effect.

CHAPTER 49

Social Currency

Most adolescents stumble through their teenage years, following trends, borrowing opinions, trying out viewpoints and assimilating the prevailing cultural whims with vehement displays of unnatural enthusiasm. If you move a teenager from one cultural environment to another, they invariably change and adapt since for most, fitting-in is the highest priority. For these individuals, much of this adaptation and transition is gradual and unconscious. For autistic individuals, for whom social interaction is a series of learned patterns and responses, this is a dangerous and frightening period. Teen culture is never static and yesterday's fashion is today's object of ridicule. For the autistic adolescent, blending in socially is always a game of catch-up with the majority, frequently revising his sets of appropriate social rules, involving constant change which is stressful and problematic. Autistic individuals require stability; teen culture never remains constant.

It is then unsurprising that individuals on the autistic spectrum often experience their greatest difficulties between the ages of 14-25. The hormonal changes at this time further contribute to their tendency to aggression or social withdrawal. Social deviancy is often the focus of peers, who are more inclined to ridicule than support.

In order to facilitate his passage at this difficult time, we invested much time, effort and money in helping him acquire social currency. No British teenager's life seems to be complete without the gaming console and accompanying mindless games which I despise with a passion. However harmless the title, to me they all seem to revolve around shooting or violence of some variety. We have carefully resisted over 18 games and grim-sounding titles but even the children's titles seem to find excuses to fight at every opportunity. For me, these are both devious and potentially corrupting and I have been known to request a refund on children's titles which belie their violent content. However, at fifteen, it is socially unacceptable to play children's games so we have had to graduate gently stepping through the minefield that is 15+ gaming. Inevitably, the difficulty and complexity of the games have increased as well, causing immense frustration and resulting aggression. I would have given up long ago but Richard, with immense patience and commitment, has spent many hours helping Ben to progress through the multitudinous layers of each game, assisted by on-line cheat codes and tips from friends. This achievement, purchased at great personal cost to my husband, buys social credibility, something to discuss with friends, a shared interest with others and a point of convergence. Perhaps it is worth it!

Mobile phones are another must-have. We introduced him to mobile technology with a simple, cheap handset, relatively easy to use and inexpensive if lost. We began with three family members as contacts and encouraged limited use. His older brother taught him to make calls using the stored numbers, then later to send simple texts. We had to teach him that calls could not be long or too frequent, with limited success. We also had to encourage him to take it when he went out as he was very fearful of losing it. Then, just before his fifteenth birthday, we purchased an i-phone, one of the more basic models of the latest technology. He was thrilled with it, delighted with the touch screen technology and the novelty of new games to play until he discovered to his disgust that his model was unable to download a new game he wanted. It is never easy to explain to an adolescent that technology is constantly being revised and improved, that today's latest gadget will soon be superseded. For Ben, this was incredulous and appalling. It took much resilience and repetition to resist his demands for an instant update. We did, despite the interminable perseverance. We knew we had no choice.

The internet is both one of the greatest tools available and a minefield of pornography and exploitation. Most of Ben's homework has involved simple fact-finding, clip art and word-processing, accessible to him through a PC, which also provides instant games, sports clips, results and music. However, when a new friend from school visited, I had to take him aside and inform him that, in my home, typing '*womin*' into images was not permissible. He cheerfully accepted my rules with a genuine "Sorry Mrs C" and adjusted his use. Fortunately, Ben was out of the room at the time, enjoying a game on his console in a parallel world.

Social media sites form an even greater danger and we resisted them entirely until Ben was approaching his fifteenth birthday. At this point, having fended off his request a million times, I felt it was time to give ground. I had never participated in these sites previously, yielding them to the younger generation. His brothers both used *Facebook* but encouraged us to desist as long as possible with Ben. What I decided to do was open up a *Facebook* page with my email as the default address. This means that all friend requests and notifications can be filtered by me before he can access them. His *Facebook* friends remain deliberately few and he enjoys exchanging messages with these contacts. It helps him to join in with the crowd and feel part of his media-driven generation. The system is not foolproof and I once intercepted a video link from a boy known to him through school with explicit pornographic images of underage girls. He never viewed these and I blocked further communication from this source but it was a clear warning to me of the dangers that lurk behind this medium.

We have frequently had to deal with the problem of Ben's repeated posts to *Facebook* friends simply saying 'Hello' each time but expecting a reply. This understandably irritates people. He does not seem to learn despite explanations from his brother, the church youth leader, teachers and ourselves.

On one occasion, we found Ben responsible for some unpleasant comments made to another pupil that he disliked. We explained that this was unacceptable and imposed a few days ban on his computer use. He said sorry to the young person. We apologised to the pupil and his parents, deleted this friend contact and discussed the incident with his school. We then endured several days on the edge of major flare-up as he reacted to his given punishment and worked through his sense of guilt. Any punishment for him is always worse for us.

On another occasion, we discovered he had purchased a hundred pounds of downloads for his mobile phone games, without realising he had done so. Fortunately, this time the company were gracious in listening to our plight and repaid the money in full. After this incident, we ensured that any downloads are made through our account, with authorisation required. These events are potentially costly. They form part of the risk incurred in investment in this form of social currency.

However, the most valuable form of social currency has been

sport. His ability to play football, table tennis, tennis, cricket and pool and his ability to run reasonably competitively have given him access to social worlds that would have been closed to him. Teenagers, it seems, will tolerate some differences if you might help their team win!

CHAPTER 50

Friendship

During his early teenage years, Ben drew immense comfort from the small group of his peers, attending the Learning Resource Base at his comprehensive school. They all had their reasons for being there. Most had also been bullied cruelly and frequently by other children because of their difficulties, yet they had a sense of camaraderie and loyalty which was precious and sustaining; they supported, encouraged and carried each other through. When we considered moving him to a special school, his friends were sad to think they might not see him again. They begged him to stay. Genuine friendships for individuals like my son are rare and precious, especially with peers who have witnessed some of his ugliest moments. Their simple acceptance and loyalty contrasted sharply with the exploitation and victimisation of others.

I was particularly touched at the poignancy of a remark by one of Ben's classmates:

"He helps me with my reading and my spelling. He is very good at that! I help him to calm down when he gets cross."

Ben's cognitive levels were probably the lowest within this group. His social interaction skills more limited than most, if not all. His behaviour at times shocking, yet they valued him, for who he *was* and for the abilities he *did* possess including his reading and spelling. In the middle of all the things Ben could not do, this individual had found something he could and invited his help in this area. It was more than an opportunity to make a contribution, it was an affirmation of value; a key building block to his self-esteem.

The ability of individuals to see the best in each other always fills me with hope and admiration. It also challenges me to re-examine my own judgements.

CHAPTER 51

Sex Education and Romance

It was lunch time and I was walking down my local high street when my mobile phone rang. It was Ben's teacher who was worried about the sex education lesson he was due to attend later that afternoon.

"I'm not sure if he's really ready to cope with the explicit nature of this teaching. What do you think?"

I smiled quietly to myself as amongst the other shoppers I knew I must be the only one discussing how to use condoms on a weekday afternoon in the high street.

"I could find him something else to do, an important job perhaps if you would prefer to have him withdrawn from the lesson. This information will be covered again in later years at school."

We agreed together that for him a delay would be helpful and he was given special duties that day. He attended later sessions but had most of his sex education in a small group with a learning assistant where the information was handled sensitively and simply. He needed information and simple explanation, far removed from the detailed curriculum of most secondary schools, at least for now.

I resumed my shopping. He enjoyed his special afternoon. As it was Friday, the others did not see him again until after the weekend. Friday afternoon's discussions were yesterday's news.

....

Then one day he returned from a special church youth event, eager, as always to tell us how the evening had progressed.

"I've just asked a girl out and she said "Yes.""

I smiled weakly, replying with a bland, vaguely positive phrase, masking the turmoil within:

"What's her name?

Inside my brain was engaged in a violent tug of war, contested by opposing emotional forces. On the one hand, I was proud of my son for having the courage to go boldly... I wanted him to enjoy every aspect of life. On the other, I was aware of the minefield we had just entered and the total unpreparedness of us both for the potential dangers ahead.

"What's she like?"

If I had ever imagined this day, it was far into a distant future, with common interests and crowded rooms and occasional holding of hands. It was with someone we had grown to know, with her family and siblings. It was certainly not a stranger, encountered in a setting where I was not present, whose background I knew nothing of.

"What school does she go to?"

He gave up answering my barrage of questions.

"I have a girlfriend." He proclaimed, proud of his achievement.

"What is she like?"

Does she know he has certain difficulties? Would it matter if she did? Does she have learning difficulties herself? This was one of those moments when you realise there are no guidebooks for being a parent and even less for having a child with additional issues. I proceeded in the only way I knew, carefully, one step at a time, aware of danger but trying not to be consumed by it...

In the event, the relationship lasted a couple of months, involved a trip to the cinema, complete with mum sitting in the foyer; a few walks in local parks and some joint youth group events. With busy lives, geography conspiring against them and limited enthusiasm from those around, the relationship naturally drifted. He had gained immense self-esteem and street-cred. We had exited the minefield for now. I was grateful to escape unscathed but aware that one day we may return, perhaps a little more prepared, hopefully in that distant future...

"Did you know there are now dating websites specifically for people with disabilities?" my neighbour chimed cheerfully one day.

'No,' I thought but then stopped. I suppose there probably are. I had never given it a thought.

"How interesting," I mumbled as my face suggested the opposite and I mechanically filed this information away in a forgotten place.

I suppose it is easy to assume, as a throw-back to a defunct age, that individuals with disabilities do not have relationships, live together, get married or have children. However, my approach to these areas was recently challenged when a young couple I know with disabilities announced their engagement. Their parents are now embarking on the uncharted path of planning a marriage where they can be supported to live together and enjoy a new freedom, within a safe framework. So far, I am thrilled for them. And children? My mind stops there, as if I cannot imagine a path through, not for everyone. Perhaps I lack the courage to go where future generations will. Perhaps. I cannot imagine my son there, not safely. Relationships, yes. Marriage maybe. That is enough for my overcrowded brain. Social norms are definitely in a state of evolution.

CHAPTER 52

Vulnerability

"Are you alone?"

When Richard casually passing the bathroom door overheard these words, he froze. He did not need all his safeguarding training to know something was not right; any parent would have known by instinct. He knocked on the door, interrupting the conversation in progress between Ben and an unknown male voice, conducted through the tablet which he held in his hand. Ben was wrapped only in a towel.

Ben was embarrassed but relieved and Richard spent the next hour or so talking to him, trying to communicate several complex concepts at a level that Ben might understand. He knew that he had to establish the facts without invading Ben's privacy; bring correction without implying guilt and instil an awareness of what is inappropriate without stifling all Ben's sexuality. For Ben, ultimately it means you do not have to do something just because you are told to do so by a friend, an adult or a stranger - something he has always found difficult to grasp. If Ben is told to do something, he would do it. He lacks the skills of discernment and differentiation between circumstances, individuals and locations. In his world of absolutes, it is difficult to create a model that is workable. Misunderstandings lead to feelings of inadequacy, frustration and distress. Richard navigates this live-ammunition battlefield with great skill. Perhaps he should have been a peace envoy. He is a skilled and much loved dad.

So it was that later that day we were sitting in our lounge helping Ben to give a formal statement to a young police officer about potential charges of sexual abuse against the voice that had emanated from his tablet via Skype. He was asked if he would be willing to testify in a court. Earlier we had contacted Ben's college as the perpetrator was another student, himself with additional needs who had previously followed the same course as Ben. This meant that in Ben's eyes, *he was a 'friend'*. Whilst Ben did not feel happy about his suggestion to take photographs and send them, he would probably have done what a 'friend' had requested. Fortunately, Richard's interception was timely. We removed this 'friend' from Ben's *Facebook* and *Skype* contacts and instructed Ben not to have anything to do with him again.

The college informed us that the student's parents had been told. They were embarrassed and apologetic - supportive individuals who had no idea what had been going on. The case never came to court, as 'no crime had been committed' partly because of a timely interception and partly because of the age of the boys, legally over the age of consent. Many questions came to mind. This law, for all the efforts of learned men and women to cover all eventualities, seems to fail in its aim to protect the vulnerable. We realised once more how difficult it will be to keep Ben safe in this multi-media world.

CHAPTER 53

Illness

Ben hates illness. He does not understand it. He cannot work out where it comes from or why it should afflict him.

"But I've done nothing wrong! Why do I get spots when that person doesn't?"

"Why have I got a cold?"

"Why does my tummy hurt when I haven't eaten too many sweets?"

I have almost given up giving logical, carefully thought-out answers. They require great effort to choose words to express complex ideas in simple language. Experience has taught me that such effort rarely produces a significant change. Fortunately, Richard with exquisite patience frequently takes on this role. Often, he is not around.

"You just have, that's all. It's not your fault. These things happen to everyone from time to time."

With feelings of guilt and failure, I move on to deal with the practical need presenting itself. Sometimes you have to move on.

His experience with members of the medical profession has been very positive. He trusts them, even regarding them as distant friends. When he has had to undergo blood tests and injections he has been very brave and when he needed stitches in a head wound, while I worried intently about how he would react, he displayed real courage.

Fortunately, Ben is rarely ill. He does however have two recurring issues, largely of his own making, that require frequent treatment. Firstly, he suffers from sore, dry skin on his lips and face, especially during the winter months. It begins with dry, cracked lips then despite treatment with topical creams in days it will spread to cover a significant area of his face. Once, someone from the school contacted me and asked me to seek medical help. Another time he required antibiotics urgently to treat the angry infection that had taken hold. The primary reason - at the first sign of soreness, he licks his lips. It is a habit he has formed and no amount of discussion and persuasion seems to help. So far from the maternal voice of protection and advice, I become the cruel mother constantly reminding him, even some unseen cause of his affliction!

It is the same with scabs. I cannot number the times I have explained the beautiful simplicity of the natural healing process yet he repeatedly removes the scabs from any cut or graze. It was with real horror that I discovered two gouged out holes at the top of his leg where he had persistently removed the protective scab layer, preventing healing and opening the wounds to the danger of infection. Anyone seeing them could be forgiven for believing him to be the object of cruelty or neglect. My first instinct was that these might need expert medical attention but in the end I settled on a technique I had used years ago for a small, deep wound I had received. I cleaned the wound, filled the holes with thick antiseptic cream and covered the area with a large dressing. He could not now access the area to remove the top layer. I kept it covered for days, changing the dressing nightly until the wounds had healed, though some scarring was inevitable. It is a technique I use frequently for lesser wounds. The spots on his face are the most difficult to deal with and he can often be seen adorned with cut-down, transparent plasters, for his own protection.

I have had to give up with his fingernails which he gnaws to the point of leaving them red and puffy, a third of the nail bed missing. It is another habit, a stress and boredom-relieving action which we have as yet failed to overcome.

Personally, I sometimes find these habits profoundly irritating - then I feel intensely guilty for doing so. As a mother, you want to love, protect, care for your child; as an individual I do not possess limitless patience or time. The result can be a potent combination of frustration and guilt. I try to resist the allure of this powerful cocktail. It would lead only to the addiction of self-pity; it could never build a fulfilling future for us both.

CHAPTER 54

Doctors, Dentists and Receptionists

Fortunately for us, Ben has had mainly positive experiences with medical staff and regards them as friends to be talked to who help you get better. This has made our dealings with them much easier than might have been the case. In fact, Ben is particularly brave in facing the regular blood testing required to monitor his medication.

What he does not cope with is conversations which might present him in a less favourable light. This makes any discussion of behavioural issues impossible without him becoming aggressive at the time or afterwards. We soon discovered that such discussions were better if he was not present and developed a system of offering him some time without us in the consulting room, particularly with the psychiatrist, giving him the freedom to say whatever he wishes. Then he waits in the waiting room while we do the same before reconvening together to discuss the way forward. This gives each of us the freedom to be honest and ultimately for progress to be made.

At my GP practice, the doctors have always made every effort to make him feel at home, listened carefully to what he has had to say and made him feel valued. Unfortunately, not all receptionists understand that I am not being difficult if I ask to see one of the doctors Ben *actually knows* or request an urgent appointment or prescription. It is a busy practice. They are often under pressure. To them, we look like any other mother and son. Sometimes I try to explain, sometimes not.

I have a high regard for my GP who has been supportive and honest throughout. Once I raised my concern about the social services taking Ben from us because they might think we were unsuitable parents. At that time, Ben sometimes *falsely* accused us of hurting him or being mean to him when he was angry with himself or a decision we had made. *We* knew the truth but would a stranger? My GP simply said that if any social worker thought of doing that, we should insist they talk to him first because he knows the whole family. He is one of the few people who know the wider picture and has seen something of the difficult times we have been through and searching decisions we have faced. His comment removed that deep fear from my mind and freed me to concentrate on the daily job in hand.

At the dentist's, Ben is proud, if a little nervous of sitting in the big chair for his regular check-up but feels he has made a great effort just by half-opening his mouth and letting the dentist move his hand mirror about. My dentist has already informed me that if he ever needs treatment, he would suggest he attends a special centre and undergoes a general anaesthetic. He is convinced that otherwise Ben would be too frightened and it would be impossible to use needles or drills safely in his mouth. What the dentist *has* done is paint his teeth with a sealant as a preventative measure and offered advice on diet and how to clean teeth effectively. Ben listens to the dietary advice but does not always follow it and continues to clean his teeth with a maximum amount of toothpaste ending up on the side of the brush head and limited efficiency in actually cleaning. When he was younger, I often helped with the job but he now feels this is unnecessary and demeaning. I frequently remind family members who encourage sticky, sweet treats that someone would have to accompany him if treatment were needed and that a general anaesthetic is undesirable for anyone, at any time, unless essential. I am no killjoy but I would not look forward to that task. Sometimes a mother's love has to sound tough!

CHAPTER 55

The New Psychiatrist

As always when facing a new doctor, I had many thoughts rushing through my head. Will he be as understanding as the last one? Will he want to change the medication or alter the dose? Will Ben cope with the change of personnel? What if Ben takes a dislike to him?

Fortunately, the run up to the appointment had been busy and time for reflection limited before the journey and the brief minutes spent in the familiar environment of the narrow waiting room. Richard and I accompanied Ben down the corridor to the consulting room. He was calm and friendly when we entered. The new psychiatrist was a large, tall man and the room felt cramped with four people in the small space. The opening conversation was routine. Ben was charming and chatty. After a while, the psychiatrist directed his gaze and questioning at Richard and me. He declared that in his opinion, medication should not be thought of as a way of controlling behaviour in teenagers. He calmly addressed us with the view that since Ben's behaviour was only difficult at home we may need to be firmer with our adolescent son. My reaction was shock and disbelief, mixed with anger. His implication seemed to be that we lacked parenting skills and the resolve to discipline Ben. Richard stared at me blankly, looking to me to reply.

I thought of Ben's large file of notes completed diligently by his former psychiatrist and wondered if this man had read any of them. I reminded him of the words 'pathological aggression linked to autism' that appeared on a recent letter from his predecessor and spoke of some of the agonies we had gone through deciding whether to accept medication. I outlined the level of aggression we had faced that had led us there. He displayed no reaction.

I informed him that we had been dealing with teenagers for thirty years in our professional capacity as teachers and had already raised two boys, now in their twenties. Whilst not being perfect parents, since they both had university degrees and clear career paths, I felt we had not done such a bad job...

The interview was soon ended. He gazed at me dispassionately and noted that I seemed to be afraid of my son and in need of support from the social services. He reluctantly agreed to recommend that Ben's case be transferred to adult services. I wondered if he was under pressure to reduce patient lists or the overall costs of that department. I thought about lodging a complaint but never did. In fact, he did refer Ben and we never saw this individual again.

Richard had to attend an appointment so we had no time together immediately after this event. I drove Ben home, engaging in cheerful, banal conversation. I did not want him to share my fury. Once home, I excused myself and drove the few minutes to the local Tesco store. Parked up outside, I called my friend.

"Hi, it's Pam. Can I scream at you for a moment please?"

Actually, it was less of a scream, which is not my expression of choice, rather a rant of "*He* said this, *I* felt that." She understood both what I felt and how important it was for me to fire this speech at someone. She gently assured me of her own view. It made me feel better and prevented me from yelling at someone else. I resumed my functional calm, determined not to allow one person's judgement to destroy my self-belief or self-control. *Perhaps that's what friends are for?*

CHAPTER 56

The Vaccination

Ben came home from college one day eager to show me a small certificate that he had been given for his vaccination. Vaccination, what vaccination? I assumed it was probably a request form until I looked at the grey card in my hand giving that day's date as when the injection was administered. Along with this card, he gave me a folded piece of paper covered in small print; the information leaflet from the individual vaccine pack and an NHS information sheet encouraging students aged 13 to 18 years to have the jab. This was the first I had heard of this programme. Ben was under the age of eighteen. I had not given consent for this. *Something was not right.*

"Did you actually have an injection today, Ben?"

"Yes. I went lunchtime and I was very brave."

"Yes, you were. Well done!" I tried not to show the concern and indignation that dominated my thoughts.

"Did anyone go with you?"

"No."

"Not even your friends?"

"No, I saw the queue by the dining hall and I joined it."

"Did you have to sign a form?"

"Yes, I did it all on my own." Ben looked for commendation and was tiring of my list of questions.

"OK. Well done."

Ben was beginning to sense he might have done something wrong. It was important to reassure him. I gave him a snack and tried to return to the usual pattern of activities.

When he went upstairs to relax, I picked up the phone and dialled the number on the card following the words 'If you have any concerns or queries…' I had several of both. I left a message with a receptionist requesting a return call from the person responsible.

As I had to wait for a response, I had time to think over what had happened which allowed my initial anger and frustration to be subjugated to reasoned thought. I concluded that I *would* have given consent for this injection, had I been consulted, which tempered my response but I recognised significant dangers inherent in the way this had been conducted: Ben would not have been able to give full details of his medication regime and if a reaction had occurred, the calmness could have quickly turned to panic, distress and a total loss of control: a response out of fear and uncertainty as much as pain or physical reaction. The nurses would have been unaware that he needed sensitive handling and some attempts to calm him, might actually have made him worse.

I then asked myself the question 'What did I want to achieve?' More than anything, I wanted to avoid a repetition of this event, not just for my son but for anyone else who is similarly vulnerable. I did not want a trophy scalp. I did not want someone to lose their job. I wanted procedural change: checks and balances to make things safer next time. A simple asterisk next to the names with a different action plan for them might be enough to alert nurses to vulnerable young people and consideration of their greater needs. Changes did not need to be complicated; only effective.

After many months had passed and feeling that my initial concerns were not being adequately addressed, I launched a formal complaint. At the end of this process, I knew that I had been listened to as procedural changes were implemented and the next time inoculations were offered at the college, the system of checks was much more robust. Progress had been made. We had all learnt from this event and could now move on.

CHAPTER 57

Respite Care

When Ben was younger, respite care was offered to us in the form of two hours a week where Ben could be looked after by a community service volunteer. These were usually young people doing a stint of voluntary work, often from abroad, so personnel changed regularly. Ben was young and at first it involved playing games with him at home or taking him to the local park in his pushchair. Sometimes the volunteer would babysit for us to go out for the evening. Some of these volunteers were warm, enthusiastic and helpful and Ben came to adore them. I can still remember a young girl from the United States and a young man from Germany whom Ben idolised. Others were clueless, like the Japanese girl who could not understand why we needed someone to look after our young disabled son *when he was asleep*. I gave up explaining and asked for a replacement.

As he grew older, the volunteers were replaced by paid carers.

These were not easy to find or keep as this role was often taken on by young people between positions and liable to move out of the area with college or new job prospects. As Ben progressed through his teens, these outings became escorted social activities such as a visit to the cinema or supported life skills training like filling in application forms for college and practice taking a bus.

Respite care always seemed to be viewed by the social services as a privilege rather than a right and at every review I feared this privilege would be taken away. Once we received a letter informing us that after a recent funding cut, our two hours a week would be withdrawn. This was reversed only after my support worker wrote a letter pleading our cause by expressing what a difference his help made to the whole family. Without this effort, we would have lost the limited help we had been given.

At our handover meeting from child to adult social care, the issue of respite came up for review and discussion. Naturally, as Ben progressed through his teens, he went to bed later and Richard and I had less time alone together. Our two other sons were living away in different parts of the country. My elderly mother lived five hours' journey away. Sometimes we needed time without Ben to spend with each other or other family members. A new respite package was agreed. It consisted of an allocated sum for an agreed number of nights of care per annum.

It sounded simple but I knew it would be not be so. I looked at the list of approved care providers, surfed the net for information and immediately rejected the cheapest on the list which had recently failed an inspection. Then I visited two of the other care providers.

The first I rejected because of a malaise I felt concerning one of the male members of staff. This was probably unfounded but the thoughts of many chilling cases of abuse by staff in similar institutions made me uneasy. It is a fine balance between mistrusting everyone and misplacing trust in apparently suitable individuals. This is impossible to judge fairly so instinct becomes the arbitrator.

The second was offering a respite care package involving taking clients to stay in small local hotels overnight. Since Ben loved hotels, the idea seemed perfect. We arranged for a taster session where he was to go out for a few hours with a helper, buy a *meal deal* from Tesco and have a walk in a nearby park or along the seafront. I decided to arrange this for a Saturday when Richard was away thinking it would break up the day. His football club had cancelled their practice that morning as it was a Bank Holiday weekend but they were meeting up in the afternoon to play snooker instead. Ben was naturally wary but ok when the lady arrived. She greeted him cheerily and declared that instead of buying a sandwich lunch she thought they might go and have a lunch at a restaurant in town, meeting up with some other clients. I was surprised at the change but since Ben loves eating out, I thought all would go smoothly. When they returned, the helper was enthusiastic and happy, saying they had had a good time. Ben was fine but quiet until she had driven off.

"Why did you make me go out with people I don't know?"

"I didn't like them."

"I didn't want to go."

"You made me go."

"They weren't very nice."

"They were loud."

"I only want to go out with my friends."

He spent the next ten minutes hating me in vivid coloured language with threats of violence. I tried to be calm. I promised him he would never have to go out with these people again. I assured him of my love, but the coiled spring had been released. The result was inevitable.

I thought that if I could get him to meet his football friends, he might be ok so we hurriedly climbed into the car. The journey would take twenty minutes. After five, I pulled the car over to the side of the road and climbed out, leaving him inside. The verbal haranguing and threats along with the kicking of the dashboard and hand movements had led me to stop. I had concluded that driving farther was unsafe.

I knew Richard was two hundred and fifty miles away. I phoned friends who lived nearby. No answer. I called another couple, living farther away. It was a Saturday. Most families were busy. Would they be out? My friend answered. Yes. Her husband was in, she would send him.

Ben was agitated. We were parked up on a busy road. Ten long minutes passed before I saw my friend's Land Rover approaching. Meanwhile their son had spoken to Ben on my mobile phone. He had accompanied his father to meet us. This young off-duty police officer took charge. He knelt beside Ben still sitting in the passenger seat, spoke calmly to him and asked him what he wanted to do next, while his father spoke to me. The options were few. We could go on to the snooker hall, go to my friends' home or return home. Even Ben realised that as time had gone on, going to the snooker hall was not a good idea. He disliked being late. He might have to explain why. He chose the option to visit my friends' house and took up the offer to ride in the Land Rover with the men. When we arrived, another visitor was already having coffee in their front room. After a few quiet, awkward moments, Ben assumed his more sociable stance and anyone arriving then might have wondered why we were there at all. After half an hour or so, we returned home to continue our day.

I analysed the day's events. It was a lot to ask Ben to go out with a stranger. It had been unwise for the carer to change the lunch plans; unwise, also to introduce other clients without warning. Autism and change produce a volatile cocktail. How much did these people really understand about autism? I was contacted later and asked for feedback. I gave it honestly and it was clear to both of us that this was not going to work for Ben now.

For a while, I did not want to think about respite care again but I knew I could not give up. Respite was about *us*, not just about *him*. There had to be a way through...

The answer came in the form of individuals that we knew. When I thought about it I could understand that Ben might not like to be escorted by a stranger. It made him feel uneasy. It made him feel different. A few months later, we employed two individuals from our church, known already to Ben. He was more relaxed from the start. After leaving him overnight with them for the first time, his words on our return were clear:

"I would like to stay with them again."

They in turn seemed to adore him. We had begun another phase of greater independence from each other. There is always an answer, if you search hard enough...

CHAPTER 58

Being Bullied and Breaking the Cycle

"Retard!"

"Thick!"

"Idiot!"

"Spastic!"

Then there are the sexually-charged expletives.

For people with disabilities, bullying is a way of life. I do not like it but in the end I have settled for a pragmatic approach:

"Ignore most things. Inform responsible adults of offensive behaviour towards you and then carry on as if nothing had happened."

It may seem defeatist but for the most part it is workable. I would like to think this approach stems from the gloating satisfaction that this way you remove from the bully their sense of triumph. I fear its origin is more having been ground down by this dripping water torture with a lasting ray of stubbornness left to fight. Either way, it works satisfactorily for my son to engage everyday with the society of which we are all part.

Before Ben went to secondary school, he had never heard most of these words but when he is angry, he redirects them towards us as vocal bullets sprayed from his machine-gun mouth to maim, offend, kill the spirit of decency and inflict wounds of guilt and sadness. This is education in its most ugly form.

Bullying. It is never as simple as it sounds. Firstly there is the issue of intent. Was this comment actually addressed to Ben? Was it a comment overheard? Was it recent? Was it provoked consciously or unconsciously by things said or done? Was it witnessed by a reliable individual? Does anyone have the authority and ability to mete out punishment or educate the bully into a different mindset? Does anyone have the time or will to do so? Would it make any lasting difference?

However, Ben is quick to take offence, quick to judge, unaware of others' problems and indiscriminate in his condemnation. He is not a reliable judge of intent, tone of voice and facial expression. He sometimes displays an absence of time awareness such that the incident which so plagues him today may actually have taken place last week, last month, last year. As such he is regarded as an unreliable source of factual information. Yet he has a keen sense of injustice and has been mistreated, abused, let down in environments where he should have been protected. I am ashamed to be part of a society that treats its most vulnerable people this way, ashamed I have not been able to make more of a difference, unwillingly upholding the status quo.

Ben likes to do what he is told, most of the time anyway. This makes him extremely vulnerable to strangers, paedophiles and peers. On one occasion, at junior school, the boys from his class derived great pleasure from telling him to knock over the playground bin as 'a bit of a laugh.' He obediently did as he was told but when the teacher duly meted out punishment the others were nowhere to be seen. Bullying, just a different form.

Then there are the physical forms: the kicks, the shoves in the line; the tripping up as he passes; the verbal taunts and the pointing and giggling behind cupped hands.

There's the extortion: "I'll give you some sweets if you pay me," or simply," Can I have a pen, pencil, rubber?" Our family supplied most of his class with equipment at one time.

These things upset me and my family as well as Ben - though he is not always aware that he is being used. The sexual nature of many taunts offends my sense of decency. The physical and emotional bullying offends our sense of pride and value. We encourage our children to live by the Biblical principle of "Treat others how you would like them to treat you." Unfortunately, not everyone does the same. The anti-discriminatory laws, though noble in intent, fail to affect many areas of our society: there remains much to change in people's attitudes.

However, there are encouraging moments, indicators of a different future. I believe attitudes *can* change. I believe good habits can be modelled.

At the parents' evening at the end of the first year at secondary school, I sat opposite a young PE teacher and told him what I believed: that my son had real ability in this area and they had totally failed to see it. I did not say it explicitly but my inference was that they had failed to look beyond his disabilities and missed giving him an opportunity to shine in one of the few areas possible for him to do so. The young teacher looked visibly shocked and mumbled something polite about looking into this matter. To his credit, he acted on my rebuke. The next year, the PE staff began to take a keen interest in him. They assigned a learning assistant to him individually and soon found that with support, he could compete with his peers very effectively in many sports.

The respect they showed him was soon mirrored by the peer group of sporty lads. It was as if the adults had shown them that they could look beyond their initial prejudicial judgement to see an individual with sporting ability that they could relate to. After all, if he was capable of scoring goals on the football pitch, getting wickets in a cricket match and winning rubbers in a table tennis tournament, they wanted to have him on their team! For four years, Ben represented the school in these three sports. This modelling of acceptance gave the young people a new perspective. Perhaps my son was never quite 'buddies' with these boys but they afforded him a kindly acceptance and consideration. They supported him with reminders and encouragements as well as practical advice in competitions such as where to stand and who to mark. In table tennis competitions, they substituted for him when he was asked to score, without embarrassing him, knowing he would not be able to do this. I do not believe this would have happened without the adults first demonstrating their own acceptance. *Change is possible*!

CHAPTER 59

The Positive Effect

I would never have chosen for my child to live with autism and have learning difficulties but I believe that my life has been enriched by the process of learning to accept, accommodate and enjoy living with it. Most of the time.

It would have been so easy for me as a parent of two academic high flyers, one a gifted sportsman, to live in the realms of top grades, sort-after university places, competitive sports trials, well-paid jobs and the privileged circles that these provide access to. I have tasted this life. It is fine and pleasant but it is fragile. Having Ben has cast me into a parallel world where some people live their entire lives. It is a world with limited funds, a world where privilege and status count for nothing, where essentials can be the only luxuries, where today is the focus and the future uncertain.

It has changed me. I am not perfect and I have moments of indulgent self-pity, those bitter-sweet moments of what-ifs, but for the main part I have laid down my petty tantrums and embraced my present and that uncertain future. I am resolute in seeking the best possible life for my son and willing to play my part in facilitating that end. I know there are limits to what I can do. I do not think that I could cope living alone with Ben for long, but that makes me more determined than ever to help him reach a position of relative independence, perhaps in some form of sheltered living arrangement which could work for all of us. This seems the best way through for Richard and me to regain some freedom whilst helping him to attain his. It is the only way I could imagine if Richard was not around.

It has changed the way I look at others. I realised this clearly the day I witnessed a young man shouting abuse and obscenities at his father in a public car park. HIs anger and disrespect was played out in this very public arena. The shock and disapprobation of the passing public was tangible. As similar thoughts flashed across my mind, I checked myself and asked two simple questions:

"What do I know of the background to this incident?"

"Could I do anything to help?"

Then knowing I could not assist here, I made a conscious decision not to stare judgementally as the elderly ladies in the department store had done and remembering how I had felt, I moved on.

I knew then that my life with Ben had changed me. I judge less and listen more. I no longer look at the homeless, the drug-takers, alcohol dependants or debtors without a thought for how they came to be where they are and often wonder if mental health or disability has played a part in bringing them there. I volunteer in my local food bank and spend time listening to their stories, signposting them to support agencies in our town and trying to offer them hope. I serve on the pastoral team in my local church. I believe that showing compassion and listening to people is important. I know. I have seen it up close. It is always worth trying to make a difference. Who doesn't need a helping hand?

CHAPTER 60

Heroes

Sometimes it's the little things that make the difference - like the first day I ever received a gift just because I was a carer. It did not matter to me what the gift was - what mattered was that someone out there noticed and cared enough to demonstrate it. I cried.

There are many groups and individuals, both charitable and professional who have provided help and encouragement. Some of these individuals have become more like friends. Many have their own personal link with disability and caring.

Our town has a particularly strong carer's forum which offers information, support and special excursions for carers and their charges. Ben has enjoyed many outings both with us and sometimes on his own with this organisation, including annual sports days and Christmas parties at Mildenhall, sponsored by the RAF. We have particularly enjoyed their weekend breaks at a holiday camp with other families facing similar problems. There is an unspoken bond between strangers here, a warm empathy if any child displays stress or unusual behaviour and an embracing of difference. It is like breathing in pure oxygen after surviving on thin air during an ascent at altitude. For most of our lives the atmosphere of acceptance is at best thin, at worst a struggle to breathe. Here we could breathe deeply and freely, relaxed among equals.

In the early days, it was particularly helpful for us to have the support of the parent liaison service funded by our local council. This gave us practical advice and encouragement to request additional support for Ben in education and was invaluable as we started out, with little knowledge of the system and processes, feeling alone and bewildered in an unknown place. Similarly, a specialist charity helped us prepare for our tribunal hearing, providing us with access to impartial, informed legal opinion on our case. This helped us significantly as we made our decision.

We are also indebted to the charity that made Ben's wish come true to go to Disneyland Paris at one of our lowest points, when we did not have the means or opportunity to wave a magic wand for ourselves. What they offered us was so much more than a short break: it was hope, encouragement, the strength to re-arm for the next engagement.

During the last eighteen years, there have been many small acts of kindness that have given me hope, many unknown heroes I would like to thank from family and friends to professionals and strangers. It can be tempting to believe that a word, a gesture will make no difference. I believe the opposite is true: it can be the flicker of hope on a black horizon, a chink of daylight in a dark cavern or make an ordinary day better - but it always makes a difference!

A Mother's Love:
Unspoken Words to my Autistic Son

I love you dearly,
Seek the best for you,
Want you to be happy,
To find your place in the world
And know you are
Valued and wanted, always.
I would do anything to remove
The pain, hurt, confusion
Integral to your daily life,
Erase the ugly violence
That sits beside your beautiful innocence.
But such ability lies
Beyond human endeavour.
So I continue to pray for that miracle
And love you with a mother's
Unconditional love,
The only kind that works.

PART 5

Moving On

Mourning for the Future

I do not think
I am jealous of others.
Rather, I mourn for a freedom
I will not have,
A future that will not be;
A development stillborn.
Like the death of a loved one
With no memories,
Only dreams.
Like the mourning of
A childless couple,
Visions of a perfect future
Without form,
Without substance.

CHAPTER 61

What Parents Want for Their Children

If you ask new parents what they want most for their child, they almost universally say they want him or her to be happy. If you observe parents of teenagers it is easy to assume that their primary aim has become success. The priority has shifted towards attaining top grades, playing for top sporting sides, perhaps performing in established drama or singing groups or aspiring to élite universities and ultimately landing a secure, well-paid job. When you become the parent of a child with additional needs, these acquired values become irrelevant, as in the social system you now belong to these criteria for evaluating success feature little, sometimes not at all.

You have entered a world where examination success will, *if* present, have a different value. When I began on this path I had no idea that qualifications existed below the A-G GCSE qualification. I had entered a world of BTEC Entry Levels, P-Scales and participation certificates. This is a world where employment prospects are few, where optimism and hope are essential. It is a world where life skills predominate over academic qualifications and self-esteem is the primary focus. It is a place where voluntary employment is a godsend and paid employment a dream, realised by the minority.

It is also a community where you meet kind-hearted, brave individuals, often working against great odds to do the best for their children, fighting frequent battles against hostile or impoverished authorities at immense personal cost. Most are not rich. Many have been forced into voluntary exile from paid employment. All of them are tired. Some are bitter. Most are heroic and driven. It is a world none of us chose to enter yet it has become a dominant factor in our daily life.

In this world, the future has a different prospect. For many that strategic change when the parents' needs become greater than the children's will never arrive. This means that the role reversal that would normally occur in later years will never happen. It means an unforeseen legacy for other siblings. It means that independence and provision of care becomes a long-term goal for everyone's good. Incremental steps towards this aim are part of everyday life. Learning to make a cup of tea, use a shower, cut your toenails, send a text, decide what to wear and how often to wash yourself or your clothes are not automatic and may take months or years. Repetition is tedious but essential. Patience is obligatory.

Did you realise that there are eight steps to follow to heat something in a microwave even after you have read the instructions on the food packaging and assuming that you can understand both the words and figures? Or eleven involved in making a cup of tea or coffee? Can you imagine having to learn sequences of actions by rote to function in simple tasks that others around you pick up without thinking? If you can, you may then be able to comprehend how a simple change in the task list can disrupt the ability to complete it because it means you must start over again. Being a parent of a young person with autism means spending your life trying to imagine these scenarios so that you can help your child accomplish simple everyday tasks. Sometimes it also means that you just want to be in another room to find some mind space to live your own life. Parents are human!

On one of my visits to a specialist autism school, the head teacher informed me with an air of certainty and authority that none of the students in her school would ever secure paid employment. It was said with a clear motive of dispelling unreality. Inside I was repulsed by her words. It seemed to me that she had given up hope and was inviting me to do the same. I silently rejected her view and determined not to place my child under her care. I know it will be difficult. I also know a few individuals with disabilities who have succeeded against the odds in securing paid jobs. My aim is for my son to enjoy the greatest level of independence possible and for him to be employed. Initially, I imagine that this may be unpaid but I dare to hope that paid employment may follow. Time will prove who is the wiser. Meanwhile, I choose to have hope.

CHAPTER 62

Wills and Pre-nuptial Agreements
(Planning for the Future)

I have always been aware that Richard and I will not be here forever, that ultimately, we must prepare Ben for the highest degree of independence open to him but with safeguards for his own safety and that of others. What that looks like practically remains the great unknown, along with how much it would cost and where the best place would be. What is important is that we are moving, however slowly towards that target.

For us as a family, this has taken us down paths that we never dreamt we would tread. It has involved us writing and re-writing our wills. At first, we nominated family members as legal guardians for our young children but as they grew, and my son's difficulties became more apparent, we tore up the wills and began again, nominating our two older sons as soon as they both reached the age of eighteen. I often thought of asking one couple we knew in the middle years but never had the courage... Can you really expect others to care for your autistic child, even your own relatives or friends? My other sons know that we *do not* expect them to have their brother to live with them. We *do* expect them to ensure that he is well looked after practically and financially.

Our first thought was to divide our worldly goods equally between our children. Then realising Ben would have all his savings used on service provision, we considered disinheriting him and giving his brothers the responsibility to provide for him. This would be a risky business, involving a sense of betrayal and of great trust. It would involve legally leaving him with nothing but the goodwill of his richer siblings. It would involve reliance on those siblings whom we know to be dependable, reasonable and full of positive plans for the future but open to influences as yet unknown. The only alternative was to set up a trust fund, which we initially rejected, unwilling to see money drain away on expensive legal fees. There was no obvious choice, offering a perfect solution.

This is what led us one day to sit around the dining table with my two other sons, discussing duties expected and responsibilities required if we chose the first option, including pre-nuptial agreements to safeguard their brother's share. Add into this the fears of unforeseen dangers including greedy partners, ill health and redundancy and a picture emerges of our family scouring the horizons for many unlikely pitfalls that most people never entertain. It was difficult for my young adult sons to comprehend these problems, especially separation and divorce with the inevitable bitterness and wrangling. It also seemed so far removed from our ordinary lives, like stepping into the world of melodrama or soap opera. At this point the documents were not written, but the seeds of the idea were sown. We were all painfully aware of the need to trust each other, to refuse to take offence, to project ourselves into a future we could not predict. This is the kind of conversation that both cements and destroys relationships!

What we were clear about was the need for power of attorney, unless the intervening years were to bring the mathematical ability needed for Ben to handle his own financial affairs. This sounded straightforward now but what if one or both of my sons ends up working abroad? Perhaps in the end we will decide a trust fund is worth the fees...

We then ran through possible types of accommodation for Ben, ranging from sheltered or supported housing to living in a residential community - but the conversation was general, based on limited facts concerning both options available and his projected needs. Still we had begun the conversation, to be continued and reviewed as time goes on...

CHAPTER 63

The Trip of a Lifetime

Imagine finding yourself in the position to enjoy the trip of a lifetime, fulfil a pipedream, do something so amazingly out of character and your comfort zone, to plan it, dream it and arrange it like some millionairess with an enthusiastic, cheerful travel agent. Then imagine the moment just before you click to book, knowing that you could not go through with it, not because your adventurous spirit failed but because your plans to care for your son fell apart and your sense of duty prevailed. Imagine the fragile satisfaction of honour overwhelmed by the sense of disappointment, aware that the opportunity may have just passed for ever...

We had always planned to have a special holiday when Richard retired. It would be something different, exotic but with a mixture of relaxation, culture and adventure. When we were younger, it was a hazy dream on a distant horizon; we had no money to fuel the ideas. Then, as retirement inched closer, we inherited some money from elderly relatives who had lived a simple, happy life, spent little and saved carefully. They in their turn had dreamed of making a special voyage. They never made the journey. Instead they left their savings to our generation and our children. It always seemed sad to me that they had let the opportunity pass. Whilst they appeared happy with their choice, I knew I would not be. However, we were aware that finding suitable provision for Ben was an almost insurmountable obstacle. Still I began to dream...

Although Richard's plans to retire had often been discussed, they remained something a way off, another year, or two, perhaps, when one day I received a phone call from my middle son, then twenty-one and in his final year at university. My husband received a mirror image of this call.

"Mum, this is the last year that I will have a long summer break and I want you and Dad to do something special this summer. I will look after Ben while you are away. Just promise me you will do it and make it something really special!"

My first thought was how kind and thoughtful, how precious to see such consideration in someone who understood the implications of the offer at an age when many were thinking only of their own hedonistic pleasure. My mind rushed with images of the worst scenarios I had witnessed – Ben had once hit his brother on the head; he had recently pushed me over in the cinema foyer. Then I asked myself how I would ever live with myself if Ben seriously injured his brother. How this young man with so much to look forward to, about to graduate with good honours, looking forward to a city career that he had worked for years to attain, could have it all taken from him as a result of this kindness. Of course, we could not really accept, could we? Then I replayed the pleading in his voice. "You will accept this offer, won't you...?" I knew that he would be disappointed if we refused and as far as the eye could see, there was no possibility of another chance like this on our horizon.

I searched for a sense of right or wrong but found only clear, logical points for and against each answer in total equilibrium. Was there even a right decision? Torn between the impelling wisdom on both sides, I hedged, delayed, procrastinated. I encouraged my son to apply for summer internships as I did not want him to turn down opportunities that might give him valuable career prospects. It did not seem fair to prejudice him on our account. I also picked up some brochures from a local travel agent and started surfing the internet. I had an elderly relative in Melbourne, Australia and began to look at touring that unique country. What an amazing place, as far distant both physically and from our daily life as is possible! My son was not offered a summer internship, perhaps because his heart was elsewhere. We began to explore what might be possible; my dream began to take shape.

Richard's initial reaction was conservative and sceptical. "We can't go that far. Why don't we go somewhere in Europe?" I knew it was really a question of letting go, that in Europe we would always have our mobile phone to hand, waiting for a call, mentally ready to catch the next plane home. Gradually he came to accept that even three hours away was too much so if we made the step of going, we could go farther afield. We could possibly go to Europe when we had less time available; we would probably never have this long again. We began to think of how we could make suitable provision for Ben to be cared for.

We decided that we were willing to take up the offer. We also agreed that we did not want to leave his brother with the task of planning activities twenty-four hours a day or for them to spend all their time together. Most other possible arrangements evaporated as the year progressed. Usually, the church youth group went away on a camping trip and Ben loved going away with them. They chose not to go this year. Ben's allocated support worker resigned and moved from the area. Ben was no longer eligible to sign up for the holiday scheme at his school, which he always enjoyed. The church café where he loved to help was closing for refurbishment. We were running out of options...

It seemed too long for him to be alone with my middle son, so the only possibility was to ask many individuals to take turns but this would leave Ben feeling unwanted and confused whilst increasing the risk of things going wrong as any programme of activities was becoming more and more complicated. I felt it was not fair and I knew we would worry. We decided not to proceed. I contacted the travel agent and my aunt, explained the issues, apologised and said that we were unable to go ahead with the booking. My aunt was disappointed but kind in her response. The travel agent said they would keep our details on file but could not guarantee prices or availability if we changed our mind. I said I was sorry. I felt saddened, disappointed but I knew I had made the right decision. Maybe another time…

The reversal of our decision began with an unlikely source. One day Ben returned from school with a letter that had been issued to all the pupils in his year. It was an invitation to join a government scheme, offering three weeks of activities and projects including two separate camping trips away, designed to engage young people in physical and social challenges and encouraging them to be responsible, mature citizens: the NCS scheme. The price was minimal as the costs were heavily subsidised. There was a choice of weeks in July and August. After the second weekend at home, the group were to take part in structured activities in the vicinity which involved raising money for local charities or serving the community. It was open to all pupils, including those with additional needs.

I must have made half a dozen phone calls to various leaders of the scheme to explain my son's idiosyncrasies and additional requirements. Someone seemed to think that an extra helper could be provided for his group. This offer was later reduced to the vague promise that an additional leader *might* be added during the scheme if this was deemed necessary. This provided slim reassurance. However, to their credit, they seemed genuinely committed to the principle of inclusion. We explained the scheme to Ben and he was keen to take up the opportunity. There was the potential for things to go wrong. It was not a perfect solution but options were few and this was the best by far.

As I clicked the final confirmation of our booking, my hand was shaking, my eyes moist. This was a gamble with the highest stakes. It involved trust, delegated responsibility, faith, freedom, adventure and spending more than we had ever before on ourselves. It was travelling physically and emotionally further than we had previously been by a multiple larger than we had believed possible. I clicked to confirm. The line was crossed. There was no turning back now.

I took Ben to the designated meeting place a few days before our departure. He had been excited but suddenly looked totally overwhelmed as we reached the car park on the edge of town where about fifty teenagers and a few parents had gathered. The organisers ticked their names off the list on their clipboards and began to engage the young people in ice-breaker games to build relationships. They were arranged in circles of 15 to 20 people. The games were new to Ben. He looked bewildered, tried to join in but did not always understand the rules. He was not alone but I wondered if he already appeared different. Even his clothes seemed unfashionable as I had followed the advice to wear simple clothes suitable for camping. The others had clearly decided to ignore this wisdom and opted for a competitive catwalk parade. I wondered if I had made the right choice.

Ben climbed up the steps to the bus and sat alone at a window seat, not because he did not want company but because he did not know anyone. I hoped and prayed and wondered if he would gel with the group. The leaders assured us they would all be fine. It reminded me of the day he started school. The bus disappeared into the distance. I climbed back into my car, sat a few minutes deep in thought and then drove home.

Later that day I took a phone call from the scheme organiser. He was concerned yet business-like and clinical about Ben's ability to settle in and his aberrant behaviour. I replied calmly, concealing my myriad thoughts. Inside my head, I saw all our careful planning being laid flat as in the proverbial pack of cards. *But I knew there was no way back now.* I asked to speak to Ben. He was ok, despite some insecurity. We spoke to him several times before we left and told him that it would be great if he could do the course but if he was unhappy, he did not have to stay. We suggested that he did the first week and reviewed things at the weekend. *We never mentioned cancelling our trip.*

Richard and I spoke to our son in charge at home. We arranged that if things did not work out, he could ask a family friend to collect Ben and bring him back to our house. We discussed some alternative activities if this happened. It would mean far greater responsibility for him if this were the case; more than we would have chosen or planned. We both knew he was ready to take up that responsibility and that he would be saddened and disappointed if we thought otherwise. The uncertainty felt like a test of our resolve to leave. *We knew we had to pass this test.*

As we stepped on board the plane at Heathrow, our adventure had begun. Richard and I thought often of the world we had left behind but for a while we lived outside of it. For the first time we actually relinquished all responsibility for our autistic son. We knew that we were so far away that even in a crisis we were not going to be much practical use. By the time we could get home, the crisis would be over and decisions would have had to be made on the ground by others. Although my mother was available for advice and consultation by phone, any practical decisions would need to be made by my other two sons, a foretaste of an inevitable distant future. *We had passed the test; we had made the right decision.*

Richard and I had a wonderful time, doing and seeing things that far exceeded my early dreams. We had stepped out of the world we had lived in for many years and landed in the world before children and responsibilities into a place of freedom and choice. We contacted them often, using email and Skype and loved hearing their news but our position was different, our viewpoint changed.

When we returned, we were pleased to be home again and prepared to return to our former world, refreshed and excited. One of the first things our middle son did was to sit us both down and give us a talk:

"Things have changed while you have been away. Ben can now do his own washing, put himself to bed, help with preparing food and put pizza and chips in the oven. You must not go back to doing these things for him. I will be disappointed if you do. I have worked to move him forward, you need to build on this, not go back!"

The irony of this role reversal brought an unseen smile to my face but I realised we had entered a changed world and we needed to heed the instructions we were given. In two and a half weeks, significant advances had been made. Not only were the two boys happy and safe but together they had forged progress at a rate that we could never have achieved. We embraced this new world order, taking up our changed role in it and following the guidelines given. We had stepped into a new phase...

CHAPTER 64

Moving on to College

Ben could only stay at his secondary school for five years. Although there was a sixth form, it had no provision for the less able. This meant that at the age of sixteen Ben and his friends would move to different colleges and sixth forms in the area. Whilst I was apprehensive of the dangers change could bring in causing him to become anxious and aggressive, I was also determined that the next major change in his life would be carefully planned well in advance and meticulously managed to minimise the impact and stress for everyone.

This was the agenda for all concerned as we convened for a 'transition planning meeting' at the beginning of Ben's last year at school. The school was fully represented at this meeting, with several staff who knew Ben and his needs well. The social worker was there too, alongside an LEA representative and a specialist transition worker, the only person there I had not previously met. The meeting was important for two reasons. Firstly, we agreed on the wording of the Learning Disability Assessment document, the legal framework for my son's educational provision into adult life. This would replace the Statement of Special Educational Needs (the Magic Key) to determine his future entitlement. Mostly it consisted of re-iterating the Statement. The discussion was open, thoughtful and decisions unanimous. Everyone knew what Ben needed and did their best to ensure that he would obtain it, including the one newcomer who helped by bringing his current knowledge of the provision available to the table.

There were two colleges locally. We put in applications to both, Ben completing his forms, helped by his support worker. The first was the main college in the centre of town. I went to visit on several occasions and Ben visited with his class on a taster day. This was the college where several of his classmates were to continue their education, though only one young girl from his group may have been in the same class. For this reason, it was probably Ben's first choice. We attended an open evening together when we were able to take a tour of the whole complex and he later attended an interview with an amiable and enthusiastic young tutor. He was offered a place.

Richard and I visited this college, observing a lesson. We asked many questions as we tried to assess the suitability of the placement. There was nothing wrong with what we saw, rather we remained unconvinced that this was the best fit for our son. What worried us most was the location, just off the main high street and open to so much greater freedom and danger than he had previously known. This was a major factor in our eventual decision to decline the offer. We did not want Ben to be different. We did not feel he was yet ready to encounter the high street!

Secondly, there was a sixth form college in the neighbouring borough offering a similar curriculum. I took a friend along to help me to form an opinion. We were both impressed. The atmosphere was caring and engaging. The curriculum was delivered around a variety of options alongside the core subjects Maths, English and ICT. The site was off a busy road but fairly self-contained. Since the nearest shops were a considerable distance away, few students ever went off-site at lunchtimes. Here he would be like everyone else. He later attended for an interview and was offered a place.

Ben was invited to a few taster days to meet his new classmates and tutors and complete some assessment tests. He emerged from the first one with a plant they had potted, the first of many attempts that we successfully grew into a sunflower, and a delicious pasty that he had made. He had enjoyed the PE fun session and met some friends from football. This combination was the perfect start and helped to allay some of his fears about our choice. He could not wait to begin!

We applied for transport provision and were accepted. This came in the form of a large taxi that picked up several students from college at agreed points along the route. The taxi driver was friendly and Ben enjoyed chatting to him. The first few mornings I walked with him to the bus stop, talking him through the journey, gradually giving him a little further to walk alone each day. After that I waved him goodbye from the house, watching him disappear into the distance, at first tentatively, then assuredly as he grew in confidence and maturity before my eyes. Ben got on well with the driver in his chatty way and arrived home on his birthday with some chocolates, a gift from him - a kind thought that made a difference.

Birthdays are special and Ben had been used to taking chocolates and cake to share in his small group at school. I could tell he wasn't sure how to approach this event at college. He was aware that things might be different but he did not know how. In the end, he took some sweets to share and wore an enormous badge I found for him saying 'It's my

307

Birthday!' Unsurprisingly, everyone noticed and made a fuss of him, singing 'Happy Birthday' as they enjoyed the sweets together. One of his tutors went to the canteen and bought them some chocolate banana cake to share. He was not sure about the banana flavour but enjoyed the attention and ate the cake anyway!

He chose animal care, hospitality, performing arts, horticulture and art and design as his options for the year, with each delivered in a block changing every half term. His first option was hospitality and before each cooking activity, the students were taken to the nearest supermarket to choose and purchase the ingredients before returning to college to cook and finally wash up. This pattern of reinforcing life skills was repeated for each option block with as many visits and activities outside of the classroom as possible, providing opportunities to gain experience in travelling on public transport and handling money. This helped the students with things many of them found difficult without drawing attention to these and making them feel embarrassed or different.

We knew Ben was happy as the change did not bring the tension that we expected. After the first week, his natural apprehension subsided. He loved going to college, enjoyed the activities of the timetabled day and warmed to the staff. Developing relationships with other students took longer but by the second term there were a few he chose regularly to spend his time with. He had begun to make new friends.

We went to the initial brief parent consultation.

"Yes, he was settling in well. No problems."

By the second consultation, all the staff knew him, and loved him.

"He is always friendly."

"Very polite."

"Makes us laugh sometimes."

"Works hard, lovely to have him."

"So enthusiastic about everything!"

"Will he be coming back next year? Great."

The first year was disappearing fast. The second was approaching. He decided to apply to stay at this college for a second year and was thrilled to find that his teachers unanimously endorsed his application.

At the end of year concert and awards evening, Ben took part in the show, singing several karaoke numbers both in a duet and part of a larger group. At the award evening that followed he was called up to the stage to receive three awards. The first was one voted by the students for being the happiest student. The second was with his team mates for representing the college at football. The last was for his 100% attendance, the only student in the unit to have attained this. He was very proud and I shared his pleasure. During the party that followed, *I* felt the awkward stranger as I barely knew anyone in the room. *He* was at the heart of the festivities, chatting to everyone, dancing and singing with both individuals and groups. He did not need me, though he wanted me to be there.

He introduced me to his girlfriend and her mother. She was sweet and proud to latch on to his arm every now and then, though Ben frequently broke away to chat to others. It seemed she was somewhat more enthusiastic than he was and at the end of the evening they parted with a brief kiss.

As I drove home that night, I knew we had made the right choice. The transition had been excellent! I also knew there would be another year to enjoy and relax before revisiting the question "Where next?"

CHAPTER 65

Coming of Age

As Ben approaches his eighteenth birthday few things in his life are changing, yet legally everything will be different. Suddenly he will be regarded as an adult with the right to vote, drink alcohol, get married and own a credit card. Suddenly, to act on his behalf, we will need special permission. Life is about to get more complicated!

Fortunately for us, Ben knows that he cannot drink alcohol with his current medication. He has never questioned this and is happy to drink diet coke in pubs and restaurants. He has witnessed a friend, with his own special needs struggle with alcohol, failing to learn the lesson of drinking too much and having to be summarily removed by his embarrassed mother from a social occasion, apparently not for the first time. Some seem to be able to drink responsibly; others may never be able to do so. Should we discourage *these* young adults from drinking at all? Should we discourage *every* young person from doing so? For now, Ben seems safe, locked in to his current custom.

Ben only handles money when he has to do so. It does not matter whether I give him a pound or a ten pound note I rarely ever see any change. Often Ben does not wait for change to be given or expect it. One day I parked outside our local Tesco and gave him the money to go and buy a meal deal (a sandwich, packet of crisps and a drink) for his lunch. I gave him a pound more than he needed as I had forgotten the exact price. I did not want him to feel flustered if he found himself short. It was the first time I had let him go shopping alone after supporting him to do so for years. He returned proudly with his lunch. He was jubilant. He had negotiated the self-checkout successfully and the receipt showed he had paid the exact price. The spare pound was nowhere to be seen. I quickly went back inside. I have no idea what happened to it, but it was gone. He was beginning to worry because he sensed my disappointment. 'Don't worry,' I said to him. 'We'll know the price for next time. You did really well!'

On a recent college trip, he had asked for money to go to MacDonald's as they had the option to have their lunch there. I gave him enough money for the Happy Meal he always ordered and had told me he would have that day. He returned home furious because they had changed their plans and eaten at Burger King where his meal had cost more. He was embarrassed as he had not had enough money. In his eyes, I was personally responsible and he was very cross with me. The same day he left his bag at college and the combination of the two events made him very edgy. In the end, we made the decision to drive the forty-minute round trip to retrieve the bag to avoid a meltdown. It was the only obvious ticket to a calmer evening.

Sometimes I feel guilty that he does not receive regular spending money and I am fearful that he has come to depend on Richard and me paying for things when he asks, expecting that this will usually happen but I do not want to see him simply lose it or waste money on unhealthy snacks and sweets as many of his friends do. He does not constantly ask for things but he is well provided for. His ability to handle money does not seem to have progressed much so it is difficult to see how it will do so. We have already signed papers concerning his disability payment to act on his behalf.

From the age of eighteen Ben will be able to vote. This both excites and frightens me. Our household follows current affairs with interest without being active in political parties at any level. Ben does not understand politics though he would recognise key national figures including the Prime Minister from the news. The idea that his actions may influence the outcome at an election is thought provoking. At one level, it is part of the enabling process and an essential part of avoiding discrimination. At another, it poses questions about the process of democracy.

Knowing that the voting process would be completely new to him, I took the opportunity of a local police commissioner election to give him a practical demonstration of how to do this. At this election, the voting numbers were extremely small as most people felt far removed from the issue and knew none of the candidates anyway. When I arrived at my polling booth, the election officers were glad to see a face just to relieve the boredom. I had Ben with me and was about to ask him to wait at the door when the idea of a voting lesson occurred to me. I asked the officers, whom I knew if it would be ok to show my son what happens when you vote. They did not see a problem so we went into the booth together and Ben watched as I marked a cross next to my chosen name on the ballot paper with the thick black crayon provided on a little piece of string. 'This is what you have to do,' I explained as I talked him through the process.

Now that we have been invited to place Ben's name on the electoral register, we have decided to request a postal vote to make it easier for him. We do not intend to make voting decisions on his behalf; the cross on the ballot paper will be his, representing his democratic right to choose. However, we will try to steer him away from extremist groups or those with stated policies that would make life harder for his future.

Credit cards will never be on our agenda for him. He is too vulnerable, the risk factor too high. I can envisage him opening his own bank account with perhaps a weekly allowance and a debit card for him to go shopping with some assistance and guidance. I know he will probably never be the most efficient shopper as the culture of tokens, special offers and discounts will be too complex for him but I foresee the day when he may shop without us with a carer alongside to assist.

We have wondered if this might be the time to take him abroad for a few days for the first time. It would have to be somewhere not too far, where the cuisine is familiar and the culture similar. Perhaps Italy where he would always find something he liked on the menu! The greatest concern would be the flight. There is nowhere to hide on a no-frills aeroplane for him or us if his ears hurt and he is frightened, distressed or aggressive. It is a gamble with high stakes. We have not yet decided whether to play this game of chance.

So as the big day approaches and we have begun to think of ways to celebrate Ben's eighteenth birthday, many ideas have flickered across my thought screen. At first, I thought of a large party at our church centre, to celebrate his eighteenth and Richard's sixtieth. This would have the advantage of including many family, friends and people from church in a familiar environment. For I while, I was excited about this possibility but then began to wonder if Ben would enjoy the combination of friends from different places brought together in an unusual mix. As time has gone on I have favoured the simpler idea of taking close family and a few friends out to the local carvery or Harvester restaurant, on familiar, predictable territory where he can enjoy the moment without too much stress. Sometimes the simple option is best.

As we approach this landmark I can look back and see how far we have come from the tough times in the beginning when we had no diagnosis and no guidelines and the early teens when Ben was unhappy and at his most aggressive. I am thankful that we are now in a better place, that we have a greater understanding of the way Ben thinks and are more able to help him avoid those situations when his frustration and stress spill over into irascibility. Whilst I am aware that we can never eliminate these moments completely, I know that when Ben is calm and happy, he can achieve many of his aspirations. My hope is that one day we will be able to look back with gratitude that he has been able to do just that!

EPILOGUE

Every now and then something breaks the sinus rhythm of life and causes us to and re-evaluate our priorities. It may be a catastrophic interruption such as the death of a relative or close friend, or the diagnosis of cancer, or it could be a lesser jolt such as being overlooked for promotion, failing a driving test, a near-miss in a car or breaking a leg, but it causes us to step back for a moment from the perpetual motion of life and look in as if from the outside. Such an incident occurred to me when I collapsed two hours into an eight-hour flight from Entebbe to Amsterdam en route for London on 6th June, 2016. I had felt unwell before boarding the plane but never anticipated what was to happen a few hours later. I came round hearing the voices of Richard, stewardesses and a retired GP who had offered his services. I was receiving oxygen from a cylinder. Whilst my first thought was to minimise the fuss and disruption, deep down I knew this was something significant.

The next six weeks passed with me living like an invalid, suffering frequent bouts of dizziness, palpitations and near-fainting episodes. I could not plan, I could not relax and significantly for Ben's life, often could not drive. I underwent various tests, saw many different doctors and watched in disbelief as all my hopes and dreams to travel, plan a new career move and enjoy life to the full seemed to disappear from view, obscured by a series of unanswered questions.

Eventually, I had a phone call at ten to five one Monday evening from a booking clerk at my local cardiology department to make an appointment for me to have a pacemaker fitted. I did not know what to say. At first I thought she had the wrong patient as no-one had mentioned this possibility to me. After clarification from the consultant, the device was fitted a couple of weeks later.

There were two points in this series of events that made me think deeply about planning for Ben's future. The first was in the early weeks when, his college having finished early for the summer, we were marooned at home, unable to do the usual things together or to make arrangements for Ben to go out with his friends as I did not know from one hour to the next how I would feel and whether I would be able to drive.

It was difficult enough for me to understand, let alone explain to an autistic mind. Suddenly I knew we must accelerate the road to independence. He must learn to travel to key places independently. It was vital for his future and had to happen as soon as possible. Sadly, I realised that this could not occur until Richard or I could ride with him to demonstrate the process. As soon as Richard was available, this was implemented and Ben now travels independently by bus to and from the church café, the food bank where he sometimes volunteers and the centre of town. It has been a big step forward.

Later, feeling groggy and mortal after the hospital treatment, I sat down and wrote a personal letter to Ben telling him how much I love him and encouraging him to be happy. It is locked in the family safe to be read when I am no longer around. I thought it would help Ben to cope with something he will not understand.

To Mum

Thank you for being kind. I love you.
Thank you for helping me.
Love from
Ben xxx

About the Author

Pam is the mother of three sons, originally from Wales but now living in South East England. After completing her secondary education at Howell's School, Llandaff, she studied French and Theatre Studies at Warwick University before training to teach Modern Languages, Drama and English to pupils from 11-18 years. Pam has continued to teach both adult and school students part-time at a variety of local schools and colleges and as a private tutor. She completed a Master's Degree in Comparative Literature when Ben was young, fitting her studies around her family and their needs. Her family has always come first but she has also tried to keep her mind alert, her body agile and a lookout for people who might need a helping hand. Pam has a strong Christian faith, combined with an impassioned love and commitment to each of her three sons and her husband of over thirty years. With every new challenge, she takes the view that there must be a way through, if you search hard enough...